STUDIES OUT IN LEFT FIELD:
DEFAMATORY ESSAYS PRESENTED TO JAMES D. MCCAWLEY

STUDIES OUT IN LEFT FIELD: DEFAMATORY ESSAYS PRESENTED TO JAMES D. McCAWLEY

ON the OCCASION Of his 33ᴿᴰ OR 34ᵗʰ BIRTHDAY

Edited by Arnold M. Zwicky
Peter H. Salus
Robert I. Binnick
Anthony L. Vanek

Reprint of the Original 1971 Edition
With a New Introduction by
Regna Darnell

John Benjamins Publishing Company
PHILADELPHIA   AMSTERDAM

Library of Congress Cataloging-in-Publication Data

Studies out in left field : defamatory essays / presented to James D.
   McCawley on the occasion of his 33rd or 34th birthday ; edited by
   Arnold M. Zwicky ... [et al.].
       p. cm.
     Originally published: Edmonton, Alta. : Champaign, Ill. :
   Linguistic Research, c1971.
     "Publications of James D. McCawley": p.
     ISBN 1-55619-460-9 (pb : alk. paper)
     1. Linguistics--Humor. 2. Words, Obscene. I. McCawley, James D.
   II. Zwicky, Arnold M.
   P26.M345S78 1992
   410'.207--dc20   92-8095
                                                     CIP

Reprinted with permission of Linguistic Research Inc.

Copyright 1992 - John Benjamins Publishing Company

Introduction

REGNA DARNELL
University of Western Ontario

I am delighted by the invitation to say a few words of appreciation on the occasion of this reprinting of one of my favourite books. Twenty-one years after its original publication, *Studies out in Left Field* is a rare book; copies are regularly stolen and those that remain are thoroughly dog-eared. For many years, I loaned my copies to my students in cultural anthropology and ethnography of speaking whose trepidation about the technicalities of linguistics was alleviated by the bawdy humour of linguists at play. What is, or at least was, the linguist's sense of humour? Ah, of course, the syntax of fucking. For the unwary would-be linguist, principles of method and formal notation seeped through along with the sampling of forbidden fruit. In spite of their humorous surface structure, many of the papers are serious pieces of linguistic analysis, grist for the mill of theory.

Re-reading the defamatory essays in 1992 takes me back to another part of my own life, a younger, freer, more innocent era, in which it was vitally important that intellectual work be *fun*. It was the era in which I first came to know Tony and Danica Vanek, and through Tony, transformational grammar and its derivatives from something akin to an insider's view.

The impetus for this reprinting is its concurrence with the publication by John Benjamins of a "real" *Festschrift* for James D. McCawley -- or at least a more conventional one. After all, Jim McCawley was only 33 (or 34, as the case may be) in 1971. He was honoured then by his peers not for a lifetime of sombre scholarship but for being first among them in sheer exuberance.

The *Preface* to the new *Festschrift* emphasizes that the group of colleagues around Jim McCawley share a conviction that "formal syntactic statements alone are not sufficient to express some fundamental and important generalizations about the grammars of natural languages." Some things, at least, have not changed. Generative Semantics has certainly produced more formal and mainstream examples and arguments. But there is an interesting continuity with the uses of language focused upon in the papers from the first *Festschrift*.

Studies out in Left Field was a group product. The 60's in North American Linguistics were a heady time. The field was small enough that everyone knew everyone else. The Linguistic Institutes of the Linguistic Society of America brought together the inner circle annually to share their humour and develop their ideas through unending conversations. There was an exuberance in the "straight" linguistics of the period too. Ideas were worked out on the blackboard and theories modified in response to far-from-passive audiences. Everybody was a student, even the gurus. We took votes about whether sentences were grammatical and revised analyses on the basis of counterexamples provided from the floor.

Transformational grammar perceived itself and was perceived by the linguistic establishment as a new thing under the sun. The rhetoric was one of scientific revolution, of discontinuity with the perceived sterility of Bloomfieldian structuralism. There were fellowships for practising academics to attend the Linguistic Institutes and learn about the new dispensation; I held one of those in 1970 and sweltered through the ethos of it all in Columbus, Ohio. The world was black and white and the good guys (including a fair number of women) were going to change it forever. And the world of linguistics *was* changed forever, though some of the old ways have returned through the back door or quietly persisted apart from the mainstream until their time came again. The new notion of grammar that began with Chomsky is frequently cited, inside and outside of the discipline of linguistics, as an example of a scientific revolution. That revolution, in our time, has reached a maintenance stage, in which there are many variations on the theory, more data is available to test the theory in its various forms, and the framework for new work seems pretty clear. This is a natural and inevitable part of the growth of a discipline or paradigm. But it doesn't have the energy of the first generation or the intensity of their social network, the sheer gusto of belonging to a group that was doing something important.

Nonetheless, the iconoclasts of the 60's have grown up. They, perhaps I should say "we", are now in positions of some institutional power. But surely part of our responsibility to the professional socialization of our own students is to convey the energy and gusto of that earlier time -- to share our memories of what it was really like. Probably no one gets all of the in-jokes in this volume. Reading over Tony Vanek's shoulder, I figure I got most of them. But the humour was intended to create solidarity, not to exclude anyone. It was possible in those days to be both iconoclastic and inclusive.

The papers in this volume began in mimeograph form, most of them composed, or at least thought out, at the Linguistic Institutes. They were circulated among the contributors. Indeed, most of the output of Chomsky's first generation of students was first produced and circulated in illegible and utterly uncopiable mimeographed versions. Things were changing too fast to wait for publication in a conventional journal.

But institutionalization comes to every new social network in intellectual life. At the end of the 60's, it was a race, at least the way Tony Vanek remembered it, whether the first issue of M.I.T.'s *Linguistic Inquiry* or his own Illinois-oriented *Papers in Linguistics* would come off the presses first. The latter was technically only one step up from the illegible mimeographs. But it made possible some unconventional publications, of which *Studies out in Left Field* was perhaps the most notable. Arnold Zwicky and Peter Salus and Bob Binnick were easily persuaded that all linguists ought to have access to the products of the defamatory insights of their colleagues and Tony Vanek made that possible.

Although the Festschrift was dedicated to Jim McCawley, I think it appropriate to say a few words about Tony Vanek too. He died in August 1987 at the age of fifty-six. He left behind a legacy of linguistic publication and research which is still with us, through Linguistic Research Inc., the Vanek Institute of Canadian Languages and Cultures, *Papers in Linguistics, The International Review of Slavic Linguistics*, and the *Current Inquiry into Language and Linguistics* monograph series. One of his passions at the time of his death was the writing of poetry by linguists, of which he encouraged publications of two volumes, with a third dedicated to his memory.

When I first met Tony Vanek, I had a lot of anthropologically-induced prejudices about transformational grammar and grammarians. I complained to him that *The Theory* (always intonationally italicized in those days) based the search for universals almost exclusively on one language, English, and failed to include the social constraints on linguistic form as part of linguistic description as such (so-called extra-linguistic rules did not, to my mind, solve the problem). I found that he studied Slavic languages, including his native Czech, and wrote a dissertation which included social features in linguistic rules, notationally as well as conceptually. I am particularly fond of the by now apocryphal story of his dissertation defense, in which an examiner who shall remain anonymous asked in consternation: "You mean you expect us to change *The Theory* on the basis of *Czech*?" Tony reported his succinct response: "Yes." Anyway, it wasn't long before I reconsidered my position about at least some TG types.

Between 1971, when this volume appeared, and 1987, Tony Vanek moved even further from the transformational grammar of his training, developing what he called the "holistic theory of human communication" and assembling a widely interdisciplinary editorial board for *Papers in Linguistics*. It was creative and experimental and iconoclastic in ways that seem to me part of the energy of that earlier period that this volume encourages us to bring to mind again. We ran a print shop in our basement. I learned how to do half-tone prints on Jim McCawley's photo for this volume. And, incessantly, we talked to people, all kinds of people. Life was never boring.

There were certainly, at the time, friends who were puzzled by Tony's directions and antagonists who were annoyed by his enthusiasms. He lost his academic position (and it remains a scandal to the discipline that he was never offered another one) because he insisted that a Slavic linguist was as much a theoretician as any other linguist, that being a linguist was a theoretical enterprise, that the study of particular languages was integral to linguistic theory. I got multiple salary increments for our joint fieldwork on Doukhobor Russian and Tony was told that the same work wasn't a contribution to Slavic linguistics because the Doukhobors of British Columbia did not speak Standard Russian. That, of course, he and I both maintained, was precisely the point. Anyway, he fought back against bureaucratic empire-building by challenging the boundaries of knowledge and discipline through his publishing enterprises and encouragement of younger scholars, as well as in his own work.

Nostalgia aside, many things have changed in two decades. This volume probably couldn't be published for the first time in 1992. Its sense of humour is indeed dated. Even in today's "politically correct" climate, however, it is still more or less OK to tell a joke if it is bracketed as a subject for analysis. Anyway, I am, more so now than then, a practising feminist, albeit without having a very formal definition of what that means. And I still think the humour in this volume is funny. It's probably important to note that a number of women laughed at and contributed to the defamatory essays (as well as to linguistics more generally). In those days, we felt we had to be twice as good as what we now call "the boys" (but that was all right because we figured we were) and at least as foul-mouthed. I wouldn't do it that way any more either. But nor would I want to impose today's standards for the respectful treatment of various "others" (women, racial minorities, aboriginal peoples, the handicapped, homosexuals, etc.) on the past. We have come a long way. Looking back at the not-so-distant past underscores that.

I assume that all readers will easily locate and probably begin with the papers on the syntax of defamatory language. Among the other pieces in this volume, I have my personal favourites. The front material tells us it is a "miracle of language" that "Finno-Ugric" survives in Siberia." Hmmm. And there is Tom Priestly's construction of a drama from the sentences linguists have used as examples. They are indeed "fragments of the collective subconscious." Many of them were deliberately ridiculous in their original citation out of context (though I have always argued that citation in a linguistic argument is in itself a specifiable and fascinating context). In any case, I honour the context of a (semi-) coherent discourse, in which it is appropriate for John's mother (isn't it nice to know that the disembodied "John" of the theoretical papers actually had a family!) to conclude that "John is stupid and Bill and Harry are similar". Finally, I cannot imagine an American Indian linguist who does not double over at the grain of truth in the generative phonology of Yakyak and its exaggeration of the conditions of fieldwork with endangered languages (to be found under the category of "Historical and Exotic"). Of course, others will have their own favourites, but that is the pleasure of the variety included in the collection.

This volume appeared in an era in which to be a linguist it seemed necessary to protest the war in Viet Nam, to write poetry, not to do fieldwork (but to use tape recorders to play music), to seek out and prepare Chinese cuisine in all its original dignity, to harness the energy of a wonderful generation of imaginative linguists toward a new understanding of language as the essence of being human. In these days, linguistics is beleaguered. We live in an anti-intellectualist society. We all too often succumb to the impulse to apologize for what we used to call "the life of the mind". Linguistic departments are succumbing to budgetary axes and we are all defensive. Perhaps it helps to remember the ties of humour and theoretical energy which have bound us over the years. There is continuity. There is solidarity. There is a shared culture which may offer us some hope for our collective future.

London, Ontario   *March 1992*

FINNO-UGRIC SURVIVES IN SIBERIA.

Charlton Laird
THE MIRACLE OF LANGUAGE

Preface

With this volume we honor the generative grammarian's Shiva, the many-handed one of transformational theory. James D. McCawley, having early abandoned chill Glasgow for windy Chicago, now decorates our Second City linguistically, politically, gastronomically, musically, and pornographically; his contributions to linguistics are equally polymorphic. In particular, he has instructed us in a style that owes as much to Lenny Bruce as it does to Leonard Bloomfield.

The Editors have been repeatedly asked: Why a Festschrift now? To which we have repeatedly replied: Why not? In addition to this overwhelming *a priori* argument, there is a practical one; observe the bibliography following this preface, and imagine what it would look like in another thirty years. Clearly, no person distinct from a major library could afford this volume in the year 2000, if it included, as it should, appropriate bibliography. And perhaps the laws on pornography will change in the meantime.

Why, then (as our more persistent inquisitors continue), McCawley's 33rd or 34th birthday? Why not choose one, for definiteness? And why not choose a nice round age, like one divisible by five? To the first question, we must plead editorial sluggishness; having failed to get this composed by March 30, 1971, we are optimistic enough to suppose that we can manage the task by March 30, 1972. As for the second question: crucial numerological considerations force us to publish before McCawley's 35th birthday. For both 33 and 34 are especially euominous numbers.

The number 33 has the prime factors of 3 and 11. The first is celebrated as a number of special import: it stands for tagmemic trimodality, for troilism, for the Trinity, for the major components of a transformational grammar, for the division of an insect's body, for the grammatical persons, for the parts of Gaul as a whole, for the dimensions of the Smith-Trager representation of English vowels, for the *menage à trois*, for the national colors of most countries, for the Fates and the judges of the underworld, for the possible phonemic vowel heights, and for the number of teaspoons in a tablespoon or feet in a yard. The number 11 is a very second-rate special number: it is sort of lucky, and it has football associations. The deep significance of 11 is that it is written with two identical strokes, i.e., that it is an icon of the number 2, and that is a mystic number -- Cartesian dualism, the *yin* and *yang*, the *yoni* and *lingam*, Jakobsonian binarism, North vs. South, left and right, binary coding, Red vs. White, the division of a spider's body, VSO or SOV, Communism vs. Capitalism, hermaphroditism, syllables or morae, to cite only a sprinkling of its manifestations.

The number 34, with prime factors 2 and 17, represents superficial (as opposed to deep) dualism in combination with perfect randomness. For no one can think of a number more random than 17. Thus, 34 stands for the precarious balance of order and chaos, of system and creativity. This balance will not be achieved again until 1989, when McCawley will be 51, and then it will be less perfect.

We have, moreover, chosen to limit this volume to contributions that are parodic, humorous, satiric, silly, obscene, or some combination of these. In this way we avoid presenting to the reader a broad mishmash of articles on Finnish, phonological theory, tone languages, generative semantics, logic, Japanese, traditional grammar, Oriental cooking, Serbo-Croatian, and English syntax. Instead, we offer a narrow mishmash of contributions which are quite unlikely to receive publication anywhere else, thanks to their content or form or both.

It is an oddity of our field, much remarked upon, that Professor McCawley, who created the interdisciplinary field of pornolinguistics and scatolinguistics virtually on his own, through enthusiastic oral communications and by generously contributing many of his spare moments, has never published a thing of this sort. Rather, he has left to the members of the inner circle (the so-called *Wienerkreis*) the dissemination of results in these areas. The *Wienerkreis*, with its epicenter in South Hanoi, has flourished under the able hands of its co-chairmen, Professors Quang Phuc Dong and Yuck Foo. These scholars, while understandably alarmed at their master's bourgeois imperialist stance in political matters, have nevertheless remained firm in their commitment to his linguistic principles. We are pleased to be able to include in this volume three of the *Wienerkreis* papers. The first of these has appeared in French translation (by M. Gross) in *Langages* 14 and in the original English in *Journal of Philosophical Linguistics* 1.2. It is reprinted here by permission of the editor of the latter journal, the so-called 'William Todd'. The second paper by Professor Quang and the squib by Professor Yuck appear in print for the first time in these pages.

The remainder of the contributions fall fairly clearly into three groups: 'hard stuff', i.e., pornolinguistics and scatolinguistics; 'soft stuff', i.e., parody and burlesque; and whimsy, which is neither obscene nor very defamatory. The reader whose sensibilities are easily injured should be guided by the section titles. Many of these pieces were composed especially for this volume, although several authors preferred to submit earlier works inspired by Professor McCawley and the *Wienerkreis*. In a few cases we have been unable to obtain highly desirable contributions; thus, the untimely demise of Orips T. Wenga of IBM and the burgeoning responsibilities of Professor Cao Dong of the University of Michigan have prevented their research from appearing here.

Some words on the contributions, their authors, and the circumstances of their composition. Behind Dr. Anantalingam, and very close to him, stands Norman Zide of the University of Chicago; his nearly unclassifiable manuscript was originally distributed, privately, in 1968. U Pani Shad's response to the early *Wienerkreis* writings was composed at about the same time; the pseudonym conceals Peter Salus of the Scarborough College of the University of Toronto, an editor of this collection. The next two contributions are the work of Cantabr-(Mass.)-igians who conspired to these ends in the spring of 1970; Munç Wang is Avery Andrews of Harvard University, and M. Tic Douloureux travels under the name of

Stephen Anderson, of the same institution. Professors Twaddle and Sweat together form Robert Binnick of the University of Kansas, also an editor of *Studies out in Left Field*; his/their article was composed especially for this volume. He is the only contributor to employ asterisks in the citation of four letter words, a convention which makes his material almost unbearably obscene. Despite this, we are publishing it, because of its timeliness. Tina Bopp is also known as Alice Davison of the State University of New York at Stony Brook.

The papers in the historical and exotic subsection were all written for this Festschrift. Renthgil is Theodore Lightner (University of Texas), seen the wrong way. Our polytechnic M. Gouet is Maurice Gross, who was visiting at Texas when he put these observations on paper. Bill Darden and Ann Zwicky have unaccountably chosen to publish their noisome works under their real names. Professor Lurba is better known as Valdis Zeps (University of Wisconsin), the editor of the only reasonably regular publication (the newsletter *Trokais Inaidniks*) to include instances of what passes for humor among linguists. Richard DeArmond (Simon Fraser University) signed his contribution with his own name. Our example of metapornolinguistics, or the use-mention confusion in real life, was written by J.R. Ross of M.I.T., under the false front of Gamahuche.

The first whimsy section contains mostly earlier works written by groups. The table of contents for *Language* was put together at the 1964 Linguistic Institute. The menu was devised in 1967, the songbook at the 1968 Linguistic Institute. The self-illustrating terminology list was composed in 1968 by a group at the University of Massachusetts under the direction of the ubiquitous U Pani Shad. The sequel was composed by Thomas Priestly (University of Alberta), also known as Fom Pop.

Ebbing Craft is the senior editor, Arnold Zwicky; the first of his articles was written at the 1968 Linguistic Institute, at the University of Illinois, the second at the 1970 Linguistic Institute, at the Ohio State University. Professor Hoke's response to the first Ebbing Craft piece is in truth the work of Paul Chapin of the University of California at San Diego. The remaining four articles in the first parody and burlesque section are new. Wm. K. Riley is, in fact, Wm. K. Riley. Cabnomme is Emmon Bach (University of Texas), if you look at him properly. Behind I.M. Cratylus lurks Adrienne Lehrer of the University of Rochester. Robert Wall was man enough to use his own name.

The second whimsy section also contains new material. Charles Fillmore's triple play on words is published orthonymously. In Professor Forthcoming Larynx-Horn it is possible to perceive Laurence Horn of the University of California at Berkeley. Detecting R.I. Binnick and (M.W. and P.H.) Salus as the anagrammatic authors of Schrimpuwskin's alphabet is more difficult.

In the final parody and burlesque section, we have Cora Rickulum, whose note on eigenvalues first appeared in the Phonetics Laboratory Notes of the University of Michigan in 1969. She has been known to teach at that university under the name of Joyce Friedman. Keith Percival is the *nom de plume* of a member of the present Washington administration who would be seriously compromised by the announcement of his real name; his

[ix]

perceptive historical analysis was composed especially to honor McCawley, and arrived at our offices in a plain brown paper. It is rumored that Joseph Voyles' Old Saxon knock-knock jokes come to us after a puzzled rejection by the editors of *Niederdeutsches Wort*.

The bibliography accompanying this preface includes only the straighter and more substantial items. We have made no attempt to compile a list of McCawley's many letters to newspapers on the subjects of linguistics, Vietnam, and pornography, for example. The Christmas story of the prince who was turned into a quadratic equation has also been omitted, as have many other enjoyable and enlightening, but ephemeral, items. We have also made no attempt to list readings of papers, although we suppose that most of these will see print eventually. Even with these severe limitations, the bibliography is an imposing one.

<u>À notre cher maître</u>, James McCawley!

March 27, 1971

A. M. Z.
P. H. S.
R. I. B.
A. L. V.

[x]

Publications of James D. McCawley

1963

Finnish Noun Morphology. *Quarterly Progress Report* 68, Research Laboratory of Electronics, M.I.T., 180-6.

Consonant Mutation in Finnish. *Quarterly Progress Report* 70, Research Laboratory of Electronics, M.I.T., 268-73.

Stress and Pitch in the Serbo-Croatian Verb. *Quarterly Progress Report* 70, Research Laboratory of Electronics, M.I.T., 282-90.

(with Jerome Kristian and Samuel A. Schmitt). Translation of Trakhtenbrot. *Algorithms and Automatic Computing Machines*. D. C. Heath.

1964

Review of Robert T. Harms, *Estonian Grammar*. *Word* 19:114-26.

1965

(with E. Wayles Browne III). Srpskohrvatski Akcenat. *Zbornik za Filologiju i Lingvistiku*.

1966

Review of Joseph Yamagiwa (ed.), *Papers of the CIC Far Eastern Language Institute*. *Language* 42:170-5.

Review of William S. Cooper, *Set Theory and Syntactic Description*. *Foundations of Language* 2:408-10.

1967

Edward Sapir's 'Phonologic Representation'. *International Journal of American Linguistics* 33:106-11.

Meaning and the Description of Languages. *Kotoba no Uchū* 2:9:10-8, 10:38-48, 11:51-57. [To be reprinted in an anthology edited by Bever and Weksel]

The Phonological Theory Behind Whitney's *Sanskrit Grammar*. *Languages and Areas: Studies Presented to George V. Bobrinskoy* (University of Chicago), 76-84.

Le Rôle d'un système de traits phonologiques dans une théorie du
langage [French translation by E. Janssens and N. Ruwet of an
unpublished English manuscript]. *Langages* 8:112-23.

1968

Can You Count Pluses and Minuses before You Can Count? *Chicago Journal
of Linguistics* 2:51-6.

The Accentuation of Japanese Noun Compounds. *Journal-Newsletter of
the Association of Teachers of Japanese.* May, 1-11.

Lexical Insertion in a Transformational Grammar without Deep Structure.
*Papers from the Fourth Regional Meeting, Chicago Linguistic
Society,* 71-80.

A Note on Faroese Vowels. *Glossa* 2:11-16.

Review of Nguyen, *English Syntax: A Combined Tagmemic-Transformational
Approach. American Anthropologist* 70:427-8.

Concerning the Base Component of a Transformational Grammar.
Foundations of Language 4:243-69.

The Phonological Component of a Grammar of Japanese. The Hague:
Mouton & Co.

The Role of Semantics in a Grammar. Bach and Harms, eds., *Universals
in Linguistic Theory.* New York: Holt, Rinehart and Winston,
124-69. [Revised version of: How to Find Semantic Universals in
the Event that there Are Any]

Review of Sebeok (ed.), *Current Trends in Linguistics,*Vol. 3
Language 44:556-93.

The Genitive Plural in Finnish. *Ural-Altaische Jahrbücher* 40:10-17.

1969

Length and Voicing in Tübatulabal. *Papers from the Fifth Regional
Meeting, Chicago Linguistic Society* 397-405.

1970

On the Applicability of *vice-versa. Linguistic Inquiry* 1:278-80.

English as a VSO Language. *Language* 46:286-99.

Review of Jespersen, *Analytic Syntax. Lanquage* 46:422-9.

Some Tonal Systems that Come Close to Being Pitch Accent Systems but Don't Quite Make It. *Papers from the Sixth Regional Meeting, Chicago Linguistic Society*, 526-32.

Meaningful Noises. *Times Literary Supplement*. July 23, 817-9.

A Note on Reflexives. *Journal of Philosophical Linguistics* 1:2:6-8.

A Note on Tone in Tiv Conjugation. *Studies in African Linguistics* 1:123-30.

Similar in that S. *Linguistic Inquiry* 1:556-9.

The Deep Structure of Negative Clauses. *Eigo Kyōiku* 19:6:72-5.

Where Do Noun Phrases Come From? Jacobs and Rosenbaum (eds.), *Readings in English Transformational Grammar*. Waltham, Mass.: Ginn. 166-83. [Part of: How to Find Semantic Universals in the Event that There Are Any]

Semantic Representation. Garvin (ed.), *Cognition: A Multiple View*. New York: Spartan Books, 227-47.

To Appear

A Programme for Logic. *Synthèse*.

Tense and Time Reference in English. Fillmore and Langendoen (eds.), *Studies in Linguistic Semantics*. New York: Holt, Rinehart and Winston.

Interpretative Semantics Meets Frankenstein. *Foundations of Language*.

William Dwight Whitney as a Syntactician. *Studies Presented to Henry and Renée Kahane*.

Review of Chomsky and Halle, *The Sound Pattern of English*. *International Journal of American Linguistics*.

Syntactic and Logical Arguments for Semantic Structures. *Proceedings of the Fifth International Seminar on Theoretical Linguistics*. Tokyo: The TEC Corporation.

Translation of Aikawa et al., *200 Chinese Recipes*.

Table of Contents

I. THE WIENERKREIS PAPERS

ENGLISH SENTENCES WITHOUT OVERT GRAMMATICAL SUBJECT[1]

QUANG PHUC DONG
South Hanoi Institute of Technology

There is an extensive literature dealing with English imperative sentences. As is well-known, these sentences have no overt grammatical subject:

(1) Close the door.

There is general agreement among scholars[2] that these sentences have deep structures involving an underlying subject *you* which is deleted by a transformation.

There is a widespread misconception that utterances such as

(2) Fuck you.

which also appear to have the form of a transitive verb followed by a noun phrase and preceded by no overt subject, are also transitive. This paper will study the syntax of sentences such as (2). While it will offer only a tentative conjecture as to what the deep structure of sentences such as (2) is, it will at least demonstrate conclusively that they are not imperatives.

One characteristic of sentences such as (2) which, as has been often noted,[3] is an anomaly if they are analyzed as imperatives, is the absence of reflexivization in (2): whereas

(3) *Assert you.

is ungrammatical, (2) is not. There are many other anomalies which are not so widely recognized. While there are a large number of structures in which imperatives appear either embedded in a matrix or with various adjuncts:

(4) I said to close the door.
(5) Don't close the door.
(6) Do close the door.
(7) Please close the door.
(8) Close the door, won't you?
(9) Go close the door.
(10) Close the door or I'll take away your teddy-bear.
(11) Close the door and I'll give you a dollar.

there are no such sentences corresponding to (2):

(12) *I said to fuck you.
(13) *Don't fuck you.
(14) *Do fuck you.
(15) *Please fuck you.

(16) *Fuck you, won't you?
(17) *Go fuck you.
(18) *Fuck you or I'll take away your teddy-bear.
(19) *Fuck you and I'll give you a dollar.

Further, while ordinary imperatives can be conjoined with each other, they cannot be conjoined with (2):

(20) Wash the dishes and sweep the floor.
(21) *Wash the dishes and fuck you.
(22) *Fuck you and wash the dishes.

Similarly, sentences such as (20) can be reduced to sentences with a conjoined verb if the two conjuncts differ only in the verb; however, the *fuck* of (2) may not appear in such a construction:

(23) Clean and press these pants.
(24) *Describe and fuck communism.

Likewise, there are sentences containing the word *fuck* which are ambiguous between a meaning parallel to (1) and a meaning parallel to (2):

(25) Fuck Lyndon Johnson.

This sentence can be interpreted either as an admonition to copulate with Lyndon Johnson or as an epithet indicating disapproval of that individual but conveying no instruction to engage in sexual relations with him. When sentences with the embeddings and adjuncts of (4) to (11) and (20) are formed, the resulting sentences allow only the former of these readings:

(12a) I said to fuck Lyndon Johnson.
(13a) Don't fuck Lyndon Johnson.
(14a) Do fuck Lyndon Johnson.
(15a) Please fuck Lyndon Johnson.
(16a) Fuck Lyndon Johnson, won't you?
(17a) Go fuck Lyndon Johnson.
(18a) Fuck Lyndon Johnson or I'll take away your teddy-bear.
(19a) Fuck Lyndon Johnson and I'll give you a dollar.
(20a) Fuck Lyndon Johnson and wash the dishes.

Consideration of these examples makes it fairly clear that the *fuck* of (12a)-(20a) (henceforth *fuck₁*) and the *fuck* of (2) (henceforth *fuck₂*) are two distinct homophonous lexical items. These two lexical items have totally different selectional restrictions, as is shown by the examples:

(26) Fuck these irregular verbs.
(27) *John fucked these irregular verbs.
(28) Fuck communism.
(29) *John fucked communism.

Moreover, $fuck_2$ has a peculiar restriction on the determiner of the following noun phrase, a restriction not shared by $fuck_1$, namely, that the determiner must be either definite or generic:

(30) Fuck these seven irregular verbs.
(31) Fuck irregular verbs.
(32) Fuck all irregular verbs.
(33) *Fuck seven irregular verbs.
(34) *Fuck any irregular verb.

but
(35) Fuck seven old ladies by midnight or I'll take away your teddy-bear.
(36) Fuck any old lady you see.

(the latter two involving $fuck_1$).[4] It should be noted that the word 'generic' must be interpreted in a sense such that *all* is generic (cf. example (32)) but *each* is not:

(37) *Fuck each irregular verb.

Indeed, substitution into the frame 'Fuck ____ irregular verb(s)' is an excellent diagnostic test for genericness. As example (35) makes clear, the two *fuck*'s also differ in their potential for co-occurring with adverbial elements: while (35) is normal,

(38) *Fuck you by midnight.

is not. Moreover, note the examples

(39) Fuck my sister tomorrow afternoon.
(40) *Fuck those irregular verbs tomorrow afternoon.
(41) Fuck my sister on the sofa.
(42) *Fuck communism on the sofa.
(43) Fuck my sister carefully.
(44) *Fuck complex symbols carefully.

Evidently $fuck_2$ does not allow any adverbial elements at all. This restriction suggests that $fuck_2$ not only is distinct from $fuck_1$ but indeed is not even a verb. Chomsky[5] observes that the adverbial elements of (39)-(42) are outside of the verb phrase and that only elements within the verb phrase play a role in strict subcategorization of verbs. That principle would clearly be violated if $fuck_2$ were a verb. While the 'principle of strictly local subcategorization' proposed by Chomsky is in fact not valid in precisely that form,[6] the fact remains that no case has been reported of any English morpheme which is unambiguously a verb and which allows no adverbial elements whatever. Since the only reason which has ever been proposed for analyzing $fuck_2$ as a verb is its appearance in a construction (that of (2)) which superficially resembles an imperative but in fact is not, one must conclude that there is in fact not a scrap of evidence in favor of assigning $fuck_2$ to the class 'verb', and indeed, assigning it to that class would force the recognition of an anomalous subclass of verbs which violate otherwise completely valid generalizations about 'verbs'.

If $fuck_2$ is not a verb, then what is it? To make some headway towards answering this question, let us consider the following expressions, which have much in common with (2):

(45) Damn Lyndon Johnson.
(46) Shit on Lyndon Johnson.
(47) To hell with Lyndon Johnson.
(48) Hooray for Cristine Keeler.

These expressions likewise exclude adverbial elements and require the following noun phrase to be definite or generic:

(49) Damn those irregular verbs.
(50) *Damn those irregular verbs tomorrow.
(51) *Damn seven irregular verbs.
(52) Shit on all irregular verbs.
(53) *Shit on each irregular verb.
(54) *Hooray for an irregular verb last night.

Only rarely have hypotheses been advanced as to the deep structure of expressions such as (45)-(48). One hypothesis[7] has been that (45) has an underlying subject *God*, which is deleted. However, this proposal is untenable since it would exclude the completely acceptable sentence

(55) Damn God.

and imply the grammaticality of the non-sentence

(56) *Damn Himself.

It is interesting that in this respect *goddamn* works exactly like *damn*:

(57) Goddamn God.
(58) *Goddamn Himself.

While the assumption of a deleted subject *God* has semantic plausibility in the case of sentences such as (46) and (2), such an analysis must be rejected for the same reason as in the case of *damn*, namely the grammaticality of

(59) Fuck God.
(60) Shit on God.

and the ungrammaticality of

(61) *Fuck Himself.
(62) *Shit on Himself.

Consider now the semantics of *fuck$_2$*, *damn*, *to hell with*, *shit on*,[8] *hooray for*, etc. A sentence consisting of one of these items plus a noun phrase has neither declarative nor interrogative nor imperative meaning: one can neither deny nor 'answer' nor 'comply with' such an utterance. These utterances simply express a favorable or unfavorable attitude on the part of the speaker towards the thing or things denoted by the noun phrase. The fact that they have such a semantic interpretation explains the restriction on the determiner of the noun phrase: the noun phrase must specify a thing or class of things in order for the utterance to be semantically interpretable. Note further the possibility of using most of the words in question without any following noun phrase:

(64) Fuck!
(65) Damn!
(66) Shit![9]
(67) Hooray!

These sentences indicate the attitude in question but do not specify what object that attitude is directed towards by the speaker.

The fact that sentences of the form *fuck₂* plus NP are not known to be validly analyzable as NP & VP in deep structure, the fact that they are not embeddable in any sentences,[10] and the fact that they allow none of the adjuncts which all other sentences allow, makes highly plausible the hypothesis that they should not even be analyzed as sentences: that the category 'utterance' be divided into two subcategories, 'sentence' and 'epithet' (the latter class including utterances such as (2), (46), and (64)), that only 'sentence' and not 'epithet' be embeddable within an utterance, that 'epithet' involve a lexical category of 'quasi-verbs' (this category consists of *fuck₂*, *shit on*, etc.[11]), that there be a phrase structure rule

Epithet → Quasi-verb NP

and that 'Quasi-verb' appear in no other phrase-structure rule.

In closing, I should mention certain problems which I have not dealt with and which the reader should be aware of. First there is the matter of stress in 'epithets'. I know of no non-ad-hoc treatment of the stress difference between

(71) Fúck yóu.
(72) Dámn yòu.

Moreover, quasi-verbs have a tendency to take primary stress: stress may disambiguate (63) (although the distinction is lost when contrastive stress is placed on the NP):

(73) Shít on the cârpet. (=Fuck₂ the carpet)
(74) Shît on the cárpet. (=Defecate on the carpet)

A second matter which deserves a full treatment is the process of historical change whereby normal lexical items become quasi-verbs. I conjecture that *fuck₂* arose historically from *fuck₁*, although the paucity of citations of *fuck* makes the philological validation of this conjecture difficult. However, it is clearly no accident that many quasi-verbs are homophonous with normal morphemes.

NOTES

[1] This research was supported by Grant PR-73 of the National Liberation Front Office of Strategic Research. An earlier version of this paper was read at a meeting of the Hanoi Linguistic Circle under the title "Why I can't tell you to fuck you".

[2] J.J.Katz and P.M.Postal, *An Integrated Theory of Linguistic Descriptions*

(MIT Press, 1964), pp. 74ff.; James P. Thorne, "English imperative sentences", *Journal of Linguistics* 2:69-77 (1966).

[3] Yuck Foo, "A note on English reflexives", Quarterly Progress Report No. 29 of the Research Laboratory of Experimental Theology, South Hanoi Institute of Technology (henceforth QPR of the RLET of SHIT), pp. 220-219, July 15, 1963.

[4] An exception to this generalization is provided by certain sentences with an indefinite pronoun:

Fuck anyone who doesn't like what I'am doing.

[5] *Aspects of the Theory of Syntax* (MIT Press, 1965), pp. 101ff.

[6] A criticism of this principle and of the claims which Chomsky makes about the constituent structure of the verb phrase is given in George Lakoff and John R. Ross, "Why you can't *do so* into the sink", Harvard Computation Laboratory Report NSF-17, pp. II-1 to II-11. Ross and Lakoff contest Chomsky's assertion that the manner adverb of (43) is part of the verb phrase.

[7] Barbara Hall Partee, personal communication (Nov. 29, 1962).

[8] Ambiguities are possible in sentences of the form *shit on NP*:

(63) Shit on the carpet.

may be either an expression of distaste for the carpet or an answer to the question "Where shall I shit?". The former meaning is to be understood throughout the remainder of the paper.

[9] The absence of the preposition in this example should be considered in the light of Lakoff's assertion (*On the Nature of Syntactic Irregularity*, Indiana University dissertation, 1965) that in verb-plus-preposition units the preposition is lexically a feature of the verb and is added to the noun-phrase by a 'segmentalization' transformation. Cf. Paul M. Postal, "On so-called 'pronouns' in English", Georgetown University Monograph Series on Language and Linguistics, 1966. I will argue below that $fuck_2$, etc. are not verbs. However, they apparently share some properties with verbs, namely, that of causing prepositions to be inserted by the same segmentalization rule.

[10] An apparent exception is quotations such as

(68) John said,'Fuck you'.

However, the object of verbs such as *say* not only is not restricted to be a sentence or a part thereof, but indeed is not even required to belong to the language to which the matrix sentence belongs: it may be something in a foreign language:

(69) John said,'Arma virumque canō.'

or even something consisting of non-speech sounds:

(70)   John said, (imitation of camel belching).

I do not take up here the interesting but difficult problem of deciding whether quotations involving sounds which the human vocal organs are incapable of producing (for example, a chord played FFF by a quartet of trombones) are to be considered ungrammatical or simply grammatical but non-occurring for performance reasons. This problem is of importance because it has bearing on the question of whether the (infinite) set of grammatical sentences in a language is denumerable or non-denumerable.

A more significant possible exception to the generalization that 'epithets' are not embeddable is the 'adjectival' *fucking*:

(71)   Drown that fucking cat!

It might appear that an analysis with embedded 'fuck that cat' is excluded by the restriction on determiners: one can say

(72)   I found seven fucking irregular verbs.

but not

(73)   *Fuck seven irregular verbs.

However, since Kuroda ("A note on relativization and certain related problems", *Language* 44:244-66 (1968)) has shown that relative clauses all go through an intermediate stage in which the relativized NP is made definite, that is no obstacle to the analysis. Moreover, a sentence such as (71) conveys the same attitude by the speaker towards the cat as does

(74)   Fuck that cat.

thus giving much semantic plausibility to this analysis. However, one must keep three problems in mind: (a) many quasi-verbs do not allow such a construction:

(75)   *Drown that shitting cat.

(b) there is no corresponding relative clause:

(76)   *Drown that cat which fuck.

and (c) there is a problem with the semantic interpretation of certain occurrences of *fucking* in embedded sentences, since

(77)   John says that his landlord is a fucking scoutmaster.

indicates the speaker's attitude towards scoutmasters and not John's.

[11] This is the same class of lexical items which Yuck Foo (op.cit.) designated as 'frigatives'. Note the further peculiar constraint on quasi-verbs that while epithets may be conjoined, quasi-verbs may not:

Fuck Lyndon Johnson and shit on Mao Tse Tung.
*Fuck and shit on Lyndon Johnson.

A NOTE ON CONJOINED NOUN PHRASES

QUANG PHUC DONG

South Hanoi Institute of Technology[1]

Two different proposals have been made which would relate pairs of sentences such as

(1) a. John and Harry are similar.
    b. John is similar to Harry.

According to Gleitman (1965:282), (1a) is derived from a conjoined structure also realizable as

(2) John is similar to Harry and Harry is similar to John.

Gleitman proposes that the reciprocal transformation converts this structure into a structure realizable as

(3) John and Harry are similar to each other.

and then 'The node dominating the reciprocal morpheme and everything that node dominates are deletable with certain kinds of verb [or adjective]'; the last clause has to do with the inapplicability of this putative transformation to e.g.,

(4) John and Harry are afraid of each other.

Lakoff and Peters (1966) propose an opposite direction of derivation: that (1a) is a more basic structure than (1b) and that (1b) arises from the same structure that underlies (1a) through a transformation of Conjunct-Extraposition, which moves one conjunct of a two-term[2] conjunction to the end of the verb phrase; the conjunction is realized as *to,* *from,*[3] *with,* or zero, depending on the verb or adjective.

The assumption of such a relationship is especially attractive in view of the enormous number of verbs and adjectives which can be used both intransitively with a conjoined subject and transitively with a simple subject, for example, *intersect, congruent, parallel, perpendicular, homologous, coincide, simultaneous, differ, different, unlike, (a)like, consistent, homphonous, rhyme, alliterate, compete, spar, clash, collide, collaborate, go steady, engaged, related, commit adultery, commit incest, hold hands, rub noses, play footsie, neck, pet.* Whatever is responsible for such pairs of transitive and intransitive clauses appears to be 'productive' in the sense that practically every verb or adjective in English which expresses either a symmetric relationship or a jointly performed action may be used in both ways; moreover, the few exceptions to this statement are transitive verbs such as *resemble, contradict,* and *equal,* which may not be used intransitively with conjoined subject as a full clause:

(6) a. *John and Mary resemble.
    b. John resembles Mary.

11

but which nonetheless exhibit a conjoined subject in nominalizations:

(7) The resemblance between John and Harry is striking.,

thus supporting the Lakoff-Peters analysis of *resemble* as having an underlying conjoined subject but being subject to obligatory Conjunct-Extraposition.

Unfortunately, there are apparently insuperable difficulties with
both analyses, or at least, with treating all of the above verbs and adjectives Gleitman's way or treating all of them the Lakoff-Peters way. Indeed,
there appears to be a verb which provides counterexamples to both accounts
of conjoined subjects, namely the verb *fuck*.[4] This verb can be used both
intransitively with conjoined subject and transitively:

(8) a. Albert and Gwendolyn were fucking.
     b. Albert was fucking Gwendolyn.

However, there is an interesting restriction that I have observed in many
(though far from all) speakers of English, namely, that the transitive
verb *fuck* (subject to a qualification to be discussed later) requires a
male subject:

(9) *Gwendolyn was fucking Albert.

Accordingly, the speakers who have this restriction likewise do not allow

(10) *Albert and Gwendolyn were fucking each other.,

thus making it impossible to derive (8a) according to the steps proposed
by Gleitman. Moreover, these facts also present difficulties for the
Lakoff-Peters proposal, since the speakers in question have no restriction
on the order of conjuncts in the conjoined subject of intransitive *fuck*:

(11) Gwendolyn and Albert were fucking.,

so that instead of merely allowing the second conjunct to be optionally
extraposed, as in the case of *similar*, it would be necessary to restrict
Conjunct-Extraposition to a conjunct specified as male if the verb is *fuck*
or one of its synonyms such as *screw*, *hump*, or *make love*   (but not, N.B.,
make love with or *copulate with*: with these verbs the speakers in question
have no restriction that the subject be male); if the extraposed conjunct
is required in addition to be the second conjunct, this treatment would
counter-intuitively treat (8b) as more closely related to (8a) than to (11);
if it is not restricted to be the second conjunct, (8b) would be derivable
in two ways, although there is no corresponding ambiguity.

There are much more serious objections to the Lakoff-Peters derivation. For example, Chomsky (personal communication) has rightly objected
to the summary of Lakoff-Peters presented in McCawley (1968a), where
McCawley treats

(12) a. Lionel and Margaret embraced.
      b. Lionel embraced Margaret.

as deriving from the same underlying structure; Chomsky points out that there are many cases where only one member of a pair such as (12) is grammatical:

 (13) a. The drunk embraced the lamppost.
    b. *The drunk and the lamppost embraced.

and that even when both sentences are grammatical, the intransitive but not the transitive one asserts a symmetric relation between the referents of the two noun phrases: (12a) entails

 (14) Margaret and Lionel embraced.,

but (12b) does not entail

 (15) Margaret embraced Lionel.

A similar fact has also been pointed out by Koutsoudas (personal communication): when *collide* is used intransitively with a conjoined subject it asserts that the referents of both conjuncts were in motion, whereas the transitive *collide* is noncommital as to whether the referent of the direct object was in motion:

 (16) a. The tank and the bicycle collided.
    b. The tank collided with the bicycle.

 (17) a. The truck collided with the lamppost.
    b. *The truck and the lamppost collided.

It is easy to construct innumerable such examples. For example,

 (18) a. Hubert Humphrey kissed Lyndon Johnson's ass.
    b. *Hubert Humphrey and Lyndon Johnson's ass kissed.

Some especially interesting examples can be constructed using *fuck*. For example, in a report of an act of necrophilia, only a transitive version is possible:

 (19) a. Boris was fucking Susie's corpse.
    b. *Boris and Susie's corpse were fucking.[5]

Similarly, in a report of homosexual intercourse, the two noun phrases in the transitive version are not interchangeable salva veritate:

 (22) a. Boris was fucking Lionel

does not entail

 (22) b. Lionel was fucking Boris.

Moreover, while a version with conjoined subject is possible:

 (23) Boris and Lionel were fucking.[6]

it is not semantically equivalent to a reciprocal construction; while (23) is appropriate to report a single event of homosexual intercourse,

(26) Boris and Lionel were fucking each other.

is appropriate only to report a series of such events (e.g., as an answer to the question 'What were your neighbors doing from 7PM to 5AM?'). A similar observation holds in the case of *kiss*, although here the judgment is much more subtle than in the case of *fuck*:

(27) Rex and Pauline kissed.

may be a report of a single kiss, but

(28) Rex and Pauline kissed each other.

can only be a report of at least two kisses. Moreover, while the sentences with *each other* allow a locative of specification (this useful term is introduced in Yuck Foo (1967)):

(29) Rex and Pauline kissed each other on the cheek.

(30) Boris and Lionel fucked each other up the ass.

the intransitives with conjoined subject do not:

(31) *Rex and Pauline kissed on the cheek.

(32) *Boris and Lionel fucked up the ass.

Of particular interest is the fact that when *fuck* is used intransitively in sentences of the type often said to arise through a transformation of Object Deletion (e.g., *John is eating*; see Lees (1960)), there is no restriction that the subject be male:

(33) Max spent the whole evening fucking.

(34) Cynthia spent the whole evening fucking.

(35) Max enjoys fucking.

(36) Cynthia enjoys fucking.

I conjecture that the range of items which can occur as the subject of sentences such as these coincides with the range of items that can appear as conjuncts when *fuck* is used intransitively with conjoined subject.

(37) *Cynthia's corpse spent the entire night fucking.

I tentatively propose to explain these facts in terms of the semantic notion of 'Agent'. An event of fucking may have either one or two agents;[8] speakers who reject (9) have a constraint that *fuck*, etc. have at least one male agent; sentences such as (34) have two underlying agents, one of which is an indefinite pronoun specified as 'Male', which is deleted. Since agents

must always be animate (Fillmore 1968), this analysis automatically excludes (19b, 37). Moreover, it explains why (34) is appropriate to describe the activities of a prostitute but not to report what happened to
the victim of a gang rape. Note in this connection the difference between

(38) The rapist fucked his victim five times.

(39) The rapist and his victim fucked five times.

While (38) may be a description of the rape that is alluded to, (39) would
only be appropriate to report events subsequent to the rape and suggests
that the victim became friendly with the rapist.

'Agent' is the name of a relation between a person (or persons) and
an action; as noted in numerous lectures and unpublished papers by Lakoff
and Ross, it can often be expressed by the verb *do* in English. My suggestion above thus is equivalent to setting up an underlying structure for
(8b) which has *do* for its main verb, *Albert* for its subject, and an embedded
sentence describing the action for its object. The embedded sentence may
be paraphrased roughly as 'There is fucking between Albert and Gwendolyn';
it is a one-place predicate which takes a conjoined subject. I suggested
above that the difference between (8a) and (8b) is whether *Albert* is the
sole agent or *Albert* and *Gwendolyn* are joint agents. In the absence of
reasons for doing otherwise, I will assume that setting up a conjoined
subject for *do* adequately reconstructs the notion of multiple agent. Accordingly, I propose that (8a) and (8b) differ as follows in underlying structure
(ignoring such irrelevancies as tense):

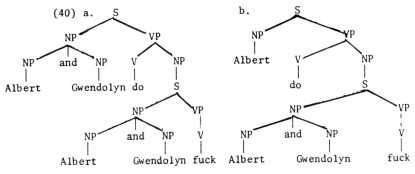

To derive (8b) from (40b), it will be necessary for there to be a transformation which is similar to the Lakoff-Peters Conjunct-Extraposition but is
obligatory rather than optional and is contingent on the next higher sentence having a subject which is identical to the first conjunct. This
transformation will obviously have to precede Equi-NP-Deletion, which must
delete the occurrence of *Albert* in the embedded clause of (40b) but cannot
apply unless conjunct extraposition has already applied.

Presumably, such a difference in underlying structures will also
be found in pairs of sentences such as

(41) Sasha, Boris, Misha, and I were playing string quartets.

(42) I was playing string quartets with Sasha, Boris and Misha.

Note that (41) cannot be derived through a derivation such as that proposed by Gleitman for (1a): first, because of the ungrammaticality of

(43) *Sasha, Boris, Misha and I were playing string quartets with each other.[9]

and secondly, because of the implausibility of the constraints which one would have to impose on sentences such as (42) to insure that the number of conjuncts in the subject and in the object of *with* added up to four.[10] Note, however, that if (42) is to be derived from an underlying structure along the lines of (40b), the revised version of Conjunct Extraposition will have to allow more than two conjuncts in the subject of the embedded sentence. As far as I can tell, the restriction of Conjunct Extraposition to two conjuncts which I alluded to in note 2 applies only to stative verbs and adjectives. I leave as an open question the problem of whether this restriction will cause different transformations to be necessary to derive sentences with statives such as *similar* than with actives such as *fuck*. The suggested revision of Conjunct Extraposition makes reference to *do* and thus would not be applicable to statives, since statives do not allow *do* as the higher underlying verb.

NOTES

[1] This research was supported in part by Grant PR-73 of the National Liberation Front Office of Strategic Research. An earlier version of this paper appeared in the QRR No. 47 of the RLET of SHIT (Quarterly Retrogress Report of the Research Laboratory of Experimental Theology of South Hanoi Institute of Technology), Jan 15, 1968, pp. 318-310. I am grateful to Rev. Quic Suc Bung for valuable comments on that version of this paper.

[2] The restriction to two-term conjunctions is necessary because of the non-synonymy of

(5) a. John, Harry and Bill are similar.
    b. John and Harry are similar to Bill.

While (5a) includes an assertion that John and Harry are similar, (5b) is non-commital about that point.

[3] The only examples I know of with *from* are *differ* and *different*.

[4] Throughout this paper I confine my attention to the true verb *fuck$_1$* and will ignore the 'quasi-verb' *fuck$_2$* (as in *Fuck Lyndon Johnson!*), which I treated in my earlier paper, Quang (1966).

[5] The only scientific or literary mention that I have found of female necrophiliacs is in a pornographic novel (Apollinaire 19) which unfortunately contains no examples similar to (19a). While some informants who reject (9) accepted analogues to (19a) that involved a female necrophiliac and a male corpse, they did so only with great reluctance and invariably added some comment such as 'It sounds odd, but that's the only way you could express it'. One other case in which these speakers accept

fuck with a female subject is in reports of lesbian acts involving a dildo; in this case the woman who is using the dildo as a substitute penis may appear as subject; indeed, under these circumstances the combination of female subject and male object is possible:

(20) Cynthia was fucking Gwendolyn with a dildo.

(21) Lady Bird was fucking Liu Shao Chi up the ass with a dildo.

[6] One unsolved problem which should be mentioned here is that despite the acceptability of (23), *bugger* does not allow a conjoined subject:

(24) a. Boris was buggering Lionel.
     b. *Boris and Lionel were buggering.

although *commit sodomy* does:

(25) a. Boris was committing sodomy with Lionel.
     b. Boris and Lionel were committing sodomy.

[7] In making these observations, I am assuming that *Boris* and *Lionel* are the names of two men. If they were the names of two snails, there would be nothing odd about using (26) to refer to a single act of (in this case, hermaphroditic) intercourse. These facts are excellent illustrations of McCawley's conclusion (1968a,b) that judgments of grammaticality and semantic oddness depend on factual knowledge and beliefs. Thus, the conclusion that (26), when it refers to two men, cannot refer to a single act of homosexual intercourse involves one's knowledge of human (as opposed to snail) anatomy and of the limits on the ability of human beings to do contortions.

[8] I ignore here sexual acts involving more than two persons. Yuck Foo (1967) convincingly defends the Jakobsonian position (pun unintentional) that all such acts can be decomposed into simultaneous binary acts.

[9] One might, however, try to salvage a Gleitman-type analysis by treating *together* as a positional variant of *with each other* and formulating some conditions under which the latter is obligatorily replaced by the former. Such a treatment might be necessary in order to explain the following data:

(44) Frog legs go well with artichokes.

(45) *Frog legs and artichokes go well.

(46) Frog legs and artichokes go well together.

[10] An interesting ambiguity in the use of *with* which I note in passing is illustrated in the sentences

(47) I was playing K. 421 with the Budapest Quartet.

(48) I was playing K. 516 with the Budapest Quartet.

(47) implies that I was a member of the Budapest Quartet, whereas (48) has two interpretations, in one of which I was a member of the Budapest Quartet,

and in the other of which I was an extra violinist who joined the Budapest Quartet to play quintets.

REFERENCES

Apollinaire, Guillaume. (19)

Bach, Emmon and Robert T. Harms. (1968). *Universals in Linguistic Theory*. New York: Holt, Rinehart & Winston.

Fillmore, Charles J. (1968) The case for case. In Bach and Harms, 1-88.

Gleitman, Lila R. (1965) Coordinating conjunctions in English. *Language* 41:260-93.

Lakoff, George, and P. Stanley Peters. (1966) Phrasal conjunction and symmetric predicates. *Mathematical Linguistics and Automatic Translation* Report NSF-17. Cambridge, Mass.: Harvard University, Computation Laboratory.

Lees, Robert B. (1960) *The Grammar of English Nominalizations.* Supplement to *International Journal of American Linguistics*. The Hague: Mouton.

McCawley, James D. (1968a) The role of semantics in a grammar. In Bach and Harms, 124-169.

McCawley, James D. (1968b) Concerning the base component of a transformational grammar. *Foundations of Language* 4:243-69.

Quang Phuc Dong. (1966) English sentences without overt grammatical subject. *Conneries Linguistiques* 19:23-31. Also in present volume.

Yuck Foo. (1967) Beitrag zur allgemeinen Stellungslehre. *Conneries Linguistiques* 20:183-219.

A SELECTIONAL RESTRICTION INVOLVING PRONOUN CHOICE[*]

YUCK FOO
South Hanoi Institute of Technology

This note is concerned with a counterexample to the outrageous claim made by the bourgeois imperialist linguist McCawley that 'there is no verb in English which allows for its subject just those noun phrases which may pronominalize to *she*, namely noun phrases denoting women, ships, and countries... selectional restrictions are definable solely in terms of properties of semantic representation' (The role of semantics in a grammar, p. 135). Consider the idiomatic sense of *shove X up Y's ass*. As is well known, Y must be coreferential to the indirect object of the next higher clause (including the deleted indirect object of a deleted performative verb):

(1) Shove it up your/*my ass.

(2) He told me to shove it up my/*your ass.

For certain speakers, X may not be a 'full' noun phrase in surface structure:

(3) Shove your foreign policy up your ass, you Yankee imperialist. (*for some speakers)

but all speakers appear to allow X to be an anaphoric pronoun:

(4) Take your foreign policy$_i$ and shove it$_i$ up your ass, you Yankee imperialist.

The pronoun may be *it* but may not be *he* or *she*:

(5) *Nixon, you imperialist butcher, take your lunatic Secretary of Defense and shove him up your ass.[1]

(6) *Nixon, you imperialist butcher, take your brainless daughter and shove her up your ass.

(7) Rockefeller, you robber baron, take your 80-foot yacht and shove it/*her up your ass.

Certain informants have reported that they find *them* acceptable but only when its antecedent is something whose singular would pronominalize to *it* rather than to *he* or *she*:

(8) *Nixon, you imperialist butcher, take your bourgeois lackeys in Taiwan and shove them up your ass.

(9) ?Nixon, you oppressor of the masses, take your anti-crime bills and shove them up your ass.

19

To the extent that these informants allow full NP's as the Y of *shove X up Y's ass*, they allow only those which pronominalize to *it* or to a *they* which would correspond to a singular *it*:

(10) *Nixon, you imperialist butcher, shove your lunatic Secretary of State up your ass.

(11) *Nixon, you imperialist butcher, shove your brainless daughter up your ass.

(12) Nixon, you oppressor of the masses, shove your anti-crime bills up your ass.

(13) *Nixon, you imperialist butcher, shove your bourgeois lackeys in Taiwan up your ass.

If (3) and (12) are grammatical but (10) and (13) ungrammatical, then the restriction on the object of *shove X up Y's ass* cannot be expressed by an output constraint and must be a constraint on deep structures, thus providing a counterexample to McCawley's claim.

NOTES

* I am grateful to the National Liberation Front for providing me with financial support and informants.

[1] The asterisk applies only to the idiomatic reading of *shove X up Y's ass*; the literal reading is grammatical but is aberrant for extra-linguistic reasons.

II. PORNOLINGUISTICS AND SCATOLINGUISTICS

A. Scatometalinguistics

'UP YOURS' AND RELATED CONSTRUCTIONS: STUDIES IN THE ENGLISH DRECATIVES I

V. ANANTALINGAM
John Lennon Reader in Indian Theoglottics,
Apologetics and Natural Language
S. A. O. S., London

à mon cher maître,
le professeur Quàng Phục Dòng

I was more than honoured to receive a form letter signed by my guru, Professor Q. P. Dồng, asking me to contribute a paper to the sixth volume of the festschrift being prepared in honor of his one hundred and fifth birthday. His continuing productivity at so ripe an age should be a lesson to us all, and the resuscitation of his famous organ[1] for the publication of these festschriften is further cause for gratulation, and for expecting its continuous publication.[2]

In this paper I am most obviously indebted to the well-known works of Jakobson, Austin, Leach, Mencken and the Sanskrit philosophers of meaning, but I owe most to the penetrating -- if not quite seminal -- paper of Dồng's 'Anal features -- phonological and syntacto-semantic -- in linguistic analysis'.[3] This paper addresses itself more directly to problems broached -- or should I say breached -- in his more recent 'English sentences without overt grammatical subjects' and to linguists interested in these fundamental problems. I ought not to fail to mention Dồng's own guru, the mysterious Maître de Port-Royal (whose name, like those of so many of the more unworldly spiritual leaders, has never been discovered) who laid the theoretical foundations for the study of our subject in his famous *De Captandi* or *On Capturing*.

On Capturing (properly *On Capturing the Logical Structure of Certain Aspects of the Notion 'Anal Component of an Expressive Grammar'*) was originally published in its fullest form (with the spectrographic analyses of Tryggar Fart) in the Genu Valgum series of Brébis (Port-Royal, 1674) but various shorter and earlier forms of sections that later went into *On Capturing* are to be found in several of the Prentiss Hall (an English monastic retreat) breviaries, catechisms and hagiographies of the period, and in the well known chapbooks *Not For Roman Jakobson* (MPR's paper is in Chuvash with a summary in Chumash) and *Not For Joshua Whatmough Either* (in Gaulish with a summary in Polish). Contemporary commentaries still of interest are those of Robertus Urbanensis (also called Palestinensis), Sidonius Agnus (also known as S. Agnus Dei), author of the once famous Reticularia, and Carolus Pottowottamicus. Also still orally available in certain monasteries are records of the Disputationes of the Confraternidad de San Diego, a dissident order of discalced Carmelites who eschewed the written word but concerned themselves endlessly with these matters.[4] Reviews of the reprint of the editio princeps (Tbilisi, 1961) -- note that various portions of this reprint in various states of vulgarization were prepublished in *Voprosy Jazykoznaniya*, Plejboj and the

Congressional Record -- of interest include those of J. McCawley (in *Parole*, formerly the *Leavenworth Linguistic Reporter*), W. von Humboldt (in *ZUMS* (*Zerschiessenheit Über Menschlichen Sprachbaues*)), Y. Malkiel (in *ARS-E* (*Anal Romance Studies-Encino*)) and Hsia Pi-Ro (in *Academia Cynica*). The spate of papers following up in one way or another these ground-breaking works -- shortage of space precludes mentioning more than a few of the more salient current trenders in analtheorie -- include R. Jakobson and M. Halle 'Tenseness and laxness', P. Strevens 'Spectra of fricative noises in human speech', N. Chowmsky 'Artesian linguistics', T. Langendoen 'The accessibility of deep (semantic) structures', various papers by Halle and associates on performance models (and somewhat similar papers by researchers at the Askins Laboratories), the recent Harvard studies of the coacquisition of word class differentiations and sphincter control, and lastly the disinterment and republication of the now justly famous paper of Meyer-Lübke and Krafft-Ebing on 'Back formations in Ibero-Romance: I (Well-formedness criteria)'.

Let me preface this study of English drecatives with a personal note, if I may. My interest in this subject, previously utterly dormant, was aroused by Professor Dồng, who was in India[5] teaching at M.I.T. (the Mangalore Institute of Theology) in 1956. I was his first and only student. We collaborated in an early survey of drecative theory and made an analysis of the major forms in my own native language. Professor Dồng also encouraged me to work in the field of child language, which I did. He directed (from Sofia, to which place he had finally gotten a visa, since, unfortunately, he was persona non grata elsewhere in Europe) my dissertation on this subject, the fieldwork (in South Carolina) for which also provided me with fieldnotes on English drecatives that I have only just begun to ransack. His own comments on my original manuscript provide rich additional attestations.

At the start, it should be clear that I use the term analtheorie (there is no English equivalent) and analtheoretical in a strictly formal sense. Some of the notions preceding and underlying the definitive formulizations were used with varying degrees of crudeness and with differing degrees of crudely interesting semitrivial results in the medieval period (see R. H. Rowbins 'Flatulatio and eructatio in medieval grammatical theory', *TPS* 99:54-198), and the postmedieval period (see N. Chowmsky 'Carthusian linguistics'), but these notions have begun to be treated formally and coherently, and without the scatological excursi that marred so much of the earlier work (see *Collected Scatological Excursi* of N. Ya. Marr) only in the past decade. In brief, analtheorie as first developed was a subbranch of partially ordered invariant subspace theory, and analtheoretical models of considerable generality and not little use were developed for econometrics in general, for sociological latticed reference group theory, and, more loosely and dubiously for history of religious analogs. The gross anatomical and grosser psychological folk usages so dear to the philosophers of natural language are completely beside any point here. The nineteenth century gave what would later be properly called analtheorie a bad name in anticipation, and this was largely through the work of one man, the Prussian anatomist Kuno von Pferdekreuz. Von Pferdekreuz in his notorious treatise *Laryngaltheorie und Analtheorie* (*Anatomische Grundlagen*, 1856, *Kulturwissenschaftliche Grundlagen,* 1889) claimed not only that the two formal theories are isomorphic in all significant respects but also that there was complete anatomic functional identity of the two organ systems, completely ignoring the cartilaginous evidence. Von Pferdekreuz' views were taken up by unscrupulous journalists and even today the pernicious nonsense begun by Pferdekreuz is not wholly dissipated. An instance of the persistence of these superceded views is to be found in the events surrounding the recent public display by the Belhl Laboratories of a new piece of software. The public that came to view this instrument, the cyclic-peristaltic extriever T-837 (known informally as the anus mirabilis) had entirely the wrong idea about the inputs and outputs of this remarkable instrument.

It will be necessary at this point to allude to the work of the only scholar who has drawn wide-ranging if shallow culturological implications from a perspective of drecativity. I am referring of course to the German primate behaviorist and Altaisant Gottnichthelf Ärschlings, now Professor of Hominid Homiletics at Berchtesgaden A. and M. The original ternary distinction drecative-precative-schrecative and the appreciation of its importance were mine, in some observations inadvertently made to Ärschlings in the Beirut bus depot in March 1958. Ärschlings rushed into print with his hastily put together *Einführung (Drecativum, Precativum and Schrecativum...)* which came out in September of that year. This was followed by his lengthy contribution to an American congress (the Woods Hole symposium on Functional Equivalents of the Shit-Eating Grin in Underdeveloped Areas), and the spate of papers in this general area by Ärschlings and his students has not stopped. Ärschlings' work is poorly written, badly organised, shows obvious and poorly digested evidences of his reading of Vico, Freud, Spengler, Sorokin, Toynbee, Sheldon, Osgood and Ringo Starr. He attempts to characterise all aspects of culture in terms of factor loadings in the three macrofactors. He has also recently introduced microfactors, and has worked out tables of factor dysplasia and factor dissonance based on universal correlational norms, established for various species, age groups, cultures, etc. He has reanalysed all of the Human Relations Area Files in his terms, and has recently launched a universal history in Drecative-Precative-Schrecative theoretic (henceforth DPS) perspective. For instance, in the low countries in the fourteenth century (according to Ärschlings and Sparafucile) agriculture was precative-precative, church law was precative-schrecative, music was drecative-precative and public administration was drecative-drecative, whereas in the fifteenth century agriculture was precative-schrecative, church law was schrecative-drecative (sic!), music was predominantly precative-precative but public administration remained drecative-drecative. Ärschlings attempts to account for these developments in terms of his tables of predicted rates and degrees of factor matrix rotation, these being calculable from his evolutionary celestial mechanical schemata. Needless to say, my own use of 'drecative', etc. is not to be confused with his, and is not emired in the theoretical confusions of Ärschlings or the formalistic models of his followers.

The Ärschlings consortium is now engaged in marinating all human knowledge in DPS theory, and is publishing several series of publications exhibiting the results of their treatment: a Series Maior on DPS theory and the physical sciences (the most recent volume is *DPS Theory and Stellar Mechanics* (Glasgow, 1967)), a Series Minor working through history (and prehistory) in DPS depth (the most recent volume being *DPS Theory and the Rise of the Mongols* (Ulan Bator, 1966)), and a Series Practica (in which the latest volume is *Does Your Base Component Have Piles, or An Intro-duction to DPS Infraposition Therapy* (Jacksonville, 1968)).

Most of Ärschlings' papers are written by his students, whom he occasionally permits to appear as recognised coauthors. His best-known collaborator is the Italian Africanist-ballerina Fiordiligi Nitti-Gritti, whose major work is her anti-Levi-Straussian polemic 'The structure of endearments in Atsi-Tatsi' (in her *Scritti Minori*, Perugia, 1959). Ärschlings himself has written comparatively little in linguistics (more narrowly defined) lately, only two papers having appeared since 1965 (*Enema and Onoma: Indogermanische Albaut und Völkerpsychologies* (*KZ* 203:198-650), and *Words for Passing Water in the Great Basin, A Study in Culture Confluence in Prehistoric America* (Conference on Ethno-Uro-Lin-guistics of the Southwest, Window Rock, 1968)).

Ärschlings most ill-advised venture -- into religionswissenschaft -- has been catastrophic. I have utterly demolished his ridiculous views in my most recent opus magnum *The Dove and the Goose, Studies in the Theo-logy of Orifical Intrusion in Western Christianity* (written in collaboration with my English disciple, L. S. D. Tordsworth, a recent convert to my school of tantric transformationalism), and they are not worth repeating here. Another student of mine has expounded my views interestingly in this connection. I refer to Gardabhedra Nath Murkhopadhyay and his signi-ficant paper *Svamātr and Paramātr in Presentday Tantric Practice in Bengal* (to appear in the forthcoming Proceedings of the Pondichery Symposium Purity, Maternity and Obscenity). My own contribution to this symposium, *La Maternité et l'Amour Courtois* (Studies in the Provençal Planhs of Gilet de Sauvetage), is of course well worth reading. These papers are parti-cularly relevant to +maternal abuse, a topic I take up later in this paper.[7][8]

(Parenthetically, it is with no little pleasure that I can announce that I have just been asked by a well-known Dutch publisher to edit his new Series Perennis (=Bibliothèque Anal) which will restore to print works on expressive language long unobtainable, and will also publish new important contributions to our science. Subscribers over twenty-one years of age will receive our monthly selections in plain wrappers directly from The Hague. With each thirty-six purchases of selections from our Series Peren-nis (or twenty-five selections from our Series Maior), the subscriber will receive absolutely free one bonus book, a selection from our Series Bonus. Among our chosen selections are:

Regina v. Lenny Bruce (London, 1969).

E. A. Hahn, *The Subjunctive as Optative in Apuleius* (Boghazköy, n.d.).

Q. P. Dong, *Drecative Universals and Universal Drecatives* (Hamburg, 1952).

J. Atzk and J. Odorf, *Readings in Systematic Theology* (Rome, 1969).

Straight from the Colon, *A Chrestomathy of Political Rhetoric 1963-1968* (Washington, 1969).

Deixis in the Lesbian Dialects (Athens, 1876).

J. Bar-Whatmough, *Praeitalic Remains* (1950).

P. J. P. Desai, *Teach Yourself Gutter Gujarati* (Ahmedabad, 1910).

Selected Context-Sensitive Behavioreme Tables from the Proxemic Atlas of Indiana: I Indianapolis 3ii, Crowded Elevators (Gary, 1966).

D. Stampe, 'The sound pattern of Comit?' (Originally published as Appendix A to *Komitski Yazyk*, Vladivostok, 1966).

II. J. K. Ward-Ronson, *An Introduction to Bulgarian Civilisation* (Skopje, 1968).

(double selection) *Shoreleave Shawnee* and *Tübatülabal for Teamsters*.

P. J. Balkanisant, *Panta Rhei: Studies in the (Linguistic) After-effects of Greek Cooking* (Athens, 1951).

P. Q. Dong and R. Rancinescu, *Cisvocatives in Bistro-Rumanian*.

V. Anantalingam, *Functional Obscenity in Algol* (reprinted from G. Tragger and P. Garrvin (eds.) *Symposium on Machine Paralanguage* (Disneyland, 1962)).

R. Parsley, T. Sage, F. H. Rosemary, and G. W. Klein, *Diglossia, A Congenital Malformation in an Eight Year Old Boy* (St. Louis. 1934).

M. A. J. Halliday, *Objurgatives in the Prose Works of Paul Postal, A Study in Rank Delicacy* (London, 1959).

T. Bullock and R. Barrett, *Radiant Heat Reception in Snakes* (Rabaul, 1910).

K. Umeboshi, R. Ajinomoto, E. Sakimuti and J. Makkori, *Sweet and Pungent Japanese* (Tokyo, 1967).

W. W. Hallo, *The Typology of Divine Exaltation* (Brooklyn, 1943).

The Dpe-rguN-dkon-pa-ḥGah-zhig-giptho-yIg of Akhu Rimpoche Śes-rab-rgya-mT sho (Lhasa, 1849).

V. Anantalingam, *Linguistic and Rhetorical Aspects of Perelmanic Discourse in Groucho Marxian Performance* (Tübingen, 1945). [This work, my habilitationsschrift, is bound together with my rehabilitationsschrift (Göttingen, 1949) which is a devastated critique of it.]

Cirencenster, J. H., *Brothel and Petrol Pump in East Anglia, A Firthian-Contextual Study of the Language of Servicing and Being Serviced in an English Town* (London, 1949).

(dual selection) E. H. Erikson, *Young Man Luther* and R. Wagner, *Mein Leben*.

The Urbana Forum on Misrules, Dysfunctions and Incompetence Models in American Dialectology (including contributions by Whicker T. Clabber, Sookie Smearcase, and V. Goober Pulleybone).

Chicago Forum on Surface Stricture and Suppository Lexical Insertion Rules.

Miami Republican Bourbonfest (complete protocols).

Catalogues are available on request.)

Careful readers of this paper will have noticed that I have not as yet gotten into its subject as announced in my title. This is pure inadvertence on my part and I promise to contain myself better in my next paper. I take it that the wellformedness of the title is its own reward, that of its readers, and sufficient justification. The material originally destined for this paper will be packaged in two other papers in the series Studies in the English Drecatives: II, Information as Faeces, and Faeces as Information, and III, Up Yours Proper, i.e., an incursus into the true subjects of Dong's imperative sentences without subjects. In this latter paper, I informally introduce the important neglected grammatical notion 'divine third person', and show the merging at a fairly deep historical and psychological level of deleted first person and deleted divine third, and discuss the resulting authority displacement and the concomitant metastasis of paratactic blasphemy.

NOTES

[1] *Conneries Linguistiques* (Nouvelle Série), 1966- (The Hague).

[2] Unfortunately, only eight days before his hundred and fifth birthday Professor Dòng was attacked by stratificationist hooligans in a Bucharest bar -- this was while he was attending the International Congress during the summer of 1967 -- and he died the next morning. His beloved journal, *CL*, as the result of an unforeseen takeover fell into the hands of Martinetian monemaniacs who gave short schrift to Dòng, and reneged on an earlier editorial promise to this writer to publish this paper. I am therefore grateful for the redacteurs of this journal for granting me the hospitality of their Xeroxed pages, thereby permitting me to honor the memory of a great linguist, nonpareil schriftseller, and much wanted agent provocateur, Quàng Phục Dòng.

[3] *Archiv Orientálni* 96:#5.

[4] I have not described the doctrinal sociology of this interesting sect not for lack of knowledge or interest, but merely because I have better things to do. Also, since the fuzz dimmed the activities of the Confraternidad, information about its current doings is harder to obtain. The infamous Vākyaracanāvilāsa (syntax orgy) at which halfcleft maenads ritual-

ly disambiguated the presanctified bourgeois formalist scapegoat limb from bloody limb to the accompaniment of hallucinogenic Bach cantatas has gine underground. (It was last performed in the West 4th Street Station of the Independent subway line.) For the sake of completeness, I shall say something about their ritual however. I get my information from the unpublished notes of an anonymous observer who is no doubt accurate to some degree in his interesting observations. The vākyaracanāvilāsa ritual opens with the singing of the two antianthems Darhe Noam and Dich, teure Halle -- sung simultaneously since no adequate motivation for any sequential ordering could be offered. This is followed by the urdrama, a Javanese shadow play, detailing obscurely the struggle of the forces of light against those of darkness. The epic is intoned in Old Javanese by a bard (or faktol) and accompanied on the gamelang by a Sarijoh. At the climax of the struggle when the bard shouts (I translate freely from the old Javanese) 'Max slices the salami with a knife, and Benny does so with a cleaver' the existential hero -- the eponymous culture-bringer Lotsap strikes the sauronic demon Tokceh with an enchanted hard salami (sharpened to a fine curare-tipped point for good measure), and Tokceh, the state of whose heart is no longer what it was, subsides (mouthing mathematical imprecations) into his pool. (Max and Benny are the Sumatran godlings of marksmanship whose blessings must be invoked in successfully aiming the fatal samali.) More about these can be learned from the standard texts of Shashibhushan Das Gupta and Ihab Hassan.

5   *Tulu Drecatives, Along with a Prolegomenon to a Theory of Drecavity.*

6   A Syntacto-Semantic Analysis of the Total Corpus of a Week's Utterances of a Top Sergeant (aged 38) in Fort Jackson, S. C., to Which is Appended a Glossary of All 659 Morphemes Used with Complete Within-Senetence Distributional Data of All Morphemes and Words. See also my M.A. Paper (done under Dong's direction) A Pikean Inventory of Behavioremes in the Kamasutra, Mangalore, 1957. I must thank the ACMS and the Ramd Corporation for supporting my study in the U.S., and also the prolonged medical treatment I was obliged to undergo before returning to India. I am also thankful to Sgt. J. J. Buck for his advice and encouragement and continuing exemplification of sentences that a foreigner often found difficult to understand. The week during which I spent twenty-four hours a day with Sgt. Buck was often difficult for both of us, and if not for his unfailing good nature the corpus could never have been satisfactorily completed. I am also grateful to a large number of bars and whorehouses -- the list is too long to quote and I hope none of these institutions will take offense -- in the Fort Jackson area for permitting me to make photomyographs, sound spectrographs and other measurements on their premises, and to the manufacturers of Jax beer, without which I should have been hard put to finish the fieldwork.

7   I don't.

9   Schrecativity has received little linguistic attention, but works of Sommerleiss and Bailey provide interesting examples of unÄrschlingsian approaches, approaches quite different from each other I must hasten to say. See Lauritz Sommerleiss 'Angstvoll, gives there a tenth rasa' (*Symposium on Sanskrit Aesthetics and Psychodynamics* (Chicago, 1945)), and C-J. Bailey (on angst) in his *Sager Studies VI* (Mauna Loa, 1970). See also his *Baileyisms and Baileyasms in Old Church Kentuckian* (Chicago, 1967).

II. PORNOLINGUISTICS AND SCATOLINGUISTICS

B. English Linguistics

SOME UNNATURAL HABITS

U PANI SHAD
Elephant's Breasts State Teachers College
of the Sacred Heart

0.   The original version of this paper[1] was written under the stimulus
        of Gorge Coughlake and Ebbing Craft during the 1968 Shambana
Summer Cuneilinguistics Festival. Many thanks for corrigenda and edentata
go to Sri Shaps, *Bnik, and Mitzi Kane. Miss Doreen Fitt was especially
helpful in providing a fertile field for "unnatural habits". This version
may only be circulated among consenting adults.

1.   In his justly famed article, Q. P. Dong[2] pointed out that *fuck* and
        several other lexical items when used in such sentences as

        (1) Fuck Lyndon Johnson.

or
        (2) Fuck you.

were not true imperatives. In a later article, Yuck Foo[3] demonstrated
that many sentences of the type

        (3) Shove X up Y's ass.

gave the lie to the bourgeois imperialist cryptolinguist McCawley, who
has claimed that "there is no verb in English which allows for its subject
just those noun phrases which may pronominalize as *she*, namely noun phrases
denoting women, ships, and countries...selectional restrictions are definable solely in terms of properties of semantic representation."[4]
Sections 2-6 of this paper will deal with Dong's forms of *fucking* and the
widespread use of *fucking*. The last section will concern Yuck Foo's
as well as Anantalingam's *drecatives*.[5]

2.   In his paper, Dong points out that *fuck* and several other lexical
        items form a[n i]discreet class of pseudo-imperatives. We will
here attempt to show that other forms of *fucking* as well as other in-
sertions (of various types and in various places) have strange and peculiar
habits. (Some imperialist lackeys of Wall Street have implied that much
of my work is making a mountain out of a *mons Veneris*, but I do not feel
it necessary to rise to this occasion nor to pierce to the heart of their
errors.)

        Sentences like

        (3) That's too bad.
        (4) That's no good.

and

        (5) That's too much.

33

are frequent in English. Similarly, emphatic forms like

> (3a) That's too fucking bad.
> (4a) That's no damn good.

and

> (5a) That's too goddam much.

may occur, though sentences like

> (3b) *That's too very bad.
> (4b) *That's no really good.

and

> (5b) *That's too blue much.

are impossible. In fact, only items we refer to as fornicatives, defecatives, and theo-imprecatives can be used in the environments *too___ADJ,
no___ADJ*,etc. We refer to this as the FORNICATORY INSERTION RULE.

This rule is limited neither in any way to American or Canadian
English, nor to the items here inserted. Even the euphemistic replacement of a fornicative or defecative permits Fornicatory Insertion. Thus,
in British English

> (6) No bloody use.
> (7) No bleeding trouble at all.

and similar locutions are in frequent use.

3.   It is commonly remarked that English does not possess infixation
        as a morphological process. Yet in Dylan Thomas's *Portrait of
the Artist as a Young Dog* we find

> (8) You can always tell a cuckoo from Bridgeend...it goes
>   cuck-BLOODY-oo, cuck-BLOODY-oo, cuck-BLOODY-oo.

and in certain linguistic strata

> (9) That's in-fucking-credible [in Québec: *in-fucking-croyable*].

occurs quite frequently. The imperialist swine James D. McCawley has been
heard to use

> (10) Christ all-fucking-mighty.

and other fornicatory data, as one would expect from a minion of the
napalm wielders.

There is no need to discuss further here the fact that again fornicatives (and their euphemistic substitutes) violate an insertion rule.

4.   There are a large number of verbs like *mess up* and *put down* which enter into such constructions as

    (11) He messes things up a lot.

and

    (12) He always puts people down.

Verbs like *fuck up*, however, are anomalous in that whereas they can be used in

    (13) He fucks things up a lot.

they also form construction like

    (14) He's a real fuck up.

whereas

    (15) *He's a real mess up.

and

    (16) *He's a real put down.

are ungrammatical. Again we find the anomaly with fornicatives. [(16) is possible in some dialects, but not with the same meaning.]

5.   Not only fornicatives and defecatives, but compounds with these word classes as one of the members can be used in the interesting ways enumerated in sections 2-4. Utterances like

    (17) That's too mother-fucking bad.

[to which exception has been raised by Sri Shaps]

    (18) Lyndon Baines mother-fucking Johnson was no worse than Tricky piss-face Dicky.

and

    (19) Spiro shit-head Agnew is the name of a venereal disease.

are more than acceptable in right-thinking circles.

6.   This mass of data collection has been attempted not only as an addendum to Maître Dong's brilliant exposition (before which I hope to prostrate myself -- or whatever else he has in mind), but also to proffer a humble suggestion: It seems to me that English fornicatives, defecatives and theo-imprecatives form a separate class of words. As can be seen from sections 1-4 there are a large number of slots which the fornicatives can enter which are blocked to other members of the same (seeming) word classes.

    We propose that this class of words be referred to as porns and that the structures in which they occur be marked [+porn].

7.   **Phonological note.** Raving McDonald (personal communication) has
pointed out in the worksheets to the *Dialect Atlas of North Eastern
American Rest-Rooms (Series Maior: Howard Johnson's Restaurants and Esso
Stations; Pt. I: Men's Rooms; Vol. 1. Connecticut and Rhode Island from
Norwalk to Providence)* that the forms with *fucking* really only arise on
the New England littoral. Elsewhere the rule

  [ŋ] → [n] / *fucki*__

is in effect.

8.   Insofar as Yuck Foo's *ass* is concerned, I feel that it has been
besmirched by Anantalingam's drecatives.

NOTES

[1] Much of the financial support for this research came from the Pontifical
Institute for the Advanced Study of the Kama Sutra, Bull-69-Paul-VI.

[2] "English sentences without overt grammatical subject"; in this volume.

[3] "A selectional restriction involving pronoun choice"; in this volume.

[4] "The role of semantics in a grammar". In Bach and Harms (eds.) *Universals in Linguistic Theory*, p. 135.

[5] "'Up yours' and related constructions: Studies in the English Drecatives
I"; in this volume.

COPULATIVE SENTENCES IN ENGLISH:
A GERMANIC LANGUAGE SPOKEN IN NORTHERN DELAWARE*

MUNÇ WANG
Socio-Linguistic Research Project
Tbilisi Institute of Tagmemics

0.   In this paper I will explore a few ins and outs of the syntax and
        semantics of copulative sentences in English, in order to present
some of the sorts of facts which must be faced by any theory which seeks
to describe the relation between the forms of sentences and their meanings.

        There is a great deal of idiolectical variation in the use of the
verbs and constructions which I shall be investigating. I will describe
the grammar of my own speech, which I have found to be not especially
bizarre with regard to these matters, although it will doubtless differ
from that of my readers at many points.

1.1   Where there is fucking, there is also an orifice at which the
        fucking is done. Hence (1a), which are equivalent, contradict
(1b), which are also equivalent:

        (1) a. Socrates fucked Xantippe.

            Socrates fucked Xantippe in some part of her body.

            b. Socrates didn't fuck Xantippe.

            Socrates fucked Xantippe in no part of her body.

        There are immensely variable constraints on the character of the
object and the location of the orifice. In my speech I find the following:
        (2) a. Butch fucked the mannikin through the hole he drilled
                in its crotch.

                Dr. Crime fucked Marjorie in the hole he had made between
                her vulva and her anus.

                Micky fucked Michelle's cadaver in its ass.

            b. ?Bret fucked the mannikin through the hole he drilled
                in its throat.

                ?Willy fucked Brenda in the mouth.

            c. *Fred fucked the log through a hole that squirrels
                had made.

In my speech the object must be the body of an animal or a reasonable
fascimile thereof, and the orifice must be located in the crotch area.

For a great many speakers this latter constraint does not exist and hence for them (2b) are grammatical.

More generally obtaining is the constraint that the orifice must be vaginoid.[1] Hence we have (3):

> (3) a. Mack fucked Fannie with a needle. [inserting it up her vagin a]
>
> b. *Patrick fucked Gwennie in a pore with a needle. [even if the pore is located in the pubic area]
>
> c. *Bradley fucked the corpse through the wound in its belly.

If no orifice is explicitly mentioned, then the vagina is assumed if the object is female, and the rectum if the object is male:

> (4) a. Achilles fucked Briseis.
>
> b. Achilles fucked Patroclus.

(4a) refers to vaginal, not rectal fucking, and even in those idiolects which allow (2b), (4b) refers to rectal, not oral fucking.

Other verbs of copulation are more restrictive than *fuck* with respect to the orifice. *Screw* must be in the vagina, and *bugger* in the rectum:

> (5) a. *Howard screwed Sylvia in the ass.
>
> b. *Jack buggered Captain Bligh in a surgically created false cunt.

Ball and *make love to* refer to vaginal intercourse, but differ from *screw* and *bugger* in rejecting explicit mention of an orifice:

> (6) a. Harold fucked Gwendolyn in her vaseline-crammed cunt.
>
> Horace screwed Alumina in her mangy twat.
>
> Theseus buggered the Minotaur in its slimy asshole.
>
> b. *Henry balled Dorothy in her luscious crotch.
>
> *Scott made love to Zelda in her brimming honey-pot.

This may be an accidental fact, or it may indicate that something deeper is going on.

Observe that when the subject is a female there is no counterpart for the male object to the orificial specification:

> (7) a. *Lucy laid Schroeder by his ten inch cock.
>
> *Dorothy laid the wizard around his big dick.

b. *Nell balled Dudley by his skinny wiener.

*Marian balled Robin Hood around his thumb.

(7b) are much worse than (6b). This is perhaps because the orificial specification is a special sort of locational complement like the prepositional phrase in *Fred kicked Mike in the balls*. Masculine intercourse with *fuck*, *screw* and *bugger* would then be construed as an action done to an object especially affecting one of its parts, parallel with such verbs as *kick*, *slug*, *punch* and *kiss*. Female intercourse, on the other hand, is seen as something done to a whole person, so that topographical considerations are irrelevant. *Ball* and *make love to* are likewise verbs of personal interaction, but when the subject is male they can reluctantly express the sort of physical-contact process found in *fuck*, *poke* and *kiss*.

In support of this it may be observed that *ball*, *make love to* and *lay* require animate objects, whereas this is much less clear with *fuck*, *screw* and *bugger*:

(8) a. Boris fucked the cadaver.

b. ?Dudley screwed the remains.

c. ?Snidely buggered the corpse.

(9) a. *The Wizard balled the witch's body.

b. *Nell laid the corpse/machine.

1.2   Where there is fucking, there is also an instrument (a tool or
       body part) with which the fucking is done. Hence (10a) are equi-
valent, and are contradictory to (10b), which are also equivalent:

(10) a. Theseus fucked Ariadne.

Theseus fucked Ariadne with something.

b. Theseus didn't fuck Ariadne.

Theseus fucked Ariadne with nothing.

If no instrument is specified, it is assumed that the penis of the subject is used, hence the first sentence of (10a) does not mean that Theseus fucked Ariadne with the Minotaur's amputated member. However, the instrument of *fuck* must always be phalloid:

(11) a. *Bartholemew fucked the princess with a dishrag.

b. Bartholemew fucked the princess with a frozen dishrag.

Constraints on what the instrument can be explain the restrictions on the sex of subjects noted in Quang (1968). *Screw* and *bugger*, which require male subjects, must be done with the subject's penis. *Lay*, which requires a female subject, must be done with the subject's vagina. *Ball*, which allows a member of either sex as its subject, merely must be done with the subject's genital organs. These facts are demonstrated in the following question-answer series:

(12) a. What do you do with your schlong?

    I fuck my sisters with it.
    I screw the nurses with it.
    I bugger choir-boys with it.
    I ball girls with it.
    *I lay newlywed brides with it.

    b. What do you do with your cunt?

    *I fuck my best students with it.
    *I screw my worst teachers with it.
    *I bugger my closer friends with it.
    I ball my patients with it.
    I lay university presidents with it.

    c. What do you do with your pencil?

    I fuck children with it.
    *I screw runaway teenie-boppers with it.
    *I bugger kiddies with it.
    *I ball nuns with it.
    *I lay monks with it.

That it is reasonable to attempt to account for the restrictions on the sex of the subjects of these verbs in terms of the restrictions on the possible instruments is well-grounded is indicated first by the fact that if a non-phallic object or body part is specified as instrument, then a female can be the subject of *fuck*:

(13) a. *Suzie fucked Gwendolyn.

    *Suzie fucked Bertie.

    b. Suzie fucked Gwendolyn with a clothespin.

    Suzie fucked Bertie up the ass with her index finger.

Secondly, it seems to me that the constraint on the instrument of *lay* can be relaxed so that an anus can serve. Then a male subject is possible:

(14) ?Bullwinkle laid Rocky.

This sentence is interpreted to mean that Rocky fucked Bullwinkle up the ass.

Unfortunately there do exist some constraints on sex which cannot be explained in terms of instruments. In many idiolects we find:

(15) a. Howard buggered Max with a dildo.

    b. *Suzie buggered Max with a dildo.

    c. *Howard buggered Suzie with a dildo.

    d. *Suzie buggered Nancy with a dildo.

For these speakers, both the subject and the object of *bugger* must be male, and the instrument may be something other than the penis of the subject.

2.   Quang (1968) proposed abstract underlying forms for both the transitive copulative construction discussed above and an intransitive construction exemplified in (16):[2]

(16) a. Jack and Jill are screwing.

    b. Popeye and Olive Oyl are fucking.

Quang maintains that in both constructions *fuck* is underlyingly a symmetric predicate FUCK embedded under an abstract verb DO as an object complement. In both constructions the subject of FUCK is an NP* containing the participants. In the intransitive construction the subject of DO is an NP* identical with the subject of FUCK, and this latter is deleted by EQUI. In the transitive construction the subject of DO is an NP identical with one of the coordinates of the subject of FUCK, and causes this coordinate to be deleted from the NP*. Predicate-Lifting of FUCK into DO and Lexicalization will then yield correct surface-structures in both cases.

Quang's position is made uncomfortable by the bahvior of the locational complements discussed in 1.1:

(17) a. Dick fucked Jane in the ass.

    b. *Dick and Jane were fucking in the ass.

(18) a. Alice kissed Jerry on the balls.

    b. *Alice and Jerry were kissing on the balls.

    c. Alice and Jerry were kissing on the lips.

By Quang's analysis, what could the locational be in deep combination with? If it were in construction with FUCK, the fact would not be accounted for that only Jane's ass, not Dick's, is affected. On the other hand it would be quite implausible to propose that the underlying subject of FUCK is *(Dick) and (Jane's ass)*, since such conjoined NP are unacceptable in surface structure.

Furthermore we cannot establish some principle to the effect that the locational pertains to the non-Agentive NP because in (18c) there are two Agents and the locational pertains to both of them.[3] It appears to be the case that a locational specification pertains to all Affected Parties. In the conjoined NP constructions the subjects are both Agents and Affected Parties, and (17b) and (18b) are unacceptable because they cannot both be affected in the specified location. In the transitive construction of (17a), however, the subject is not an Affected Party, hence the sentence is acceptable.

That this account is correct is argued by (19):

(19) Ozma and Cruella were fucking in the ass with a double-ended dildo.

Here Ozma and Cruella are posed rear-to-rear with the dildo inserted into both their assholes. The sentence is acceptable because both parties are affected where specified by the locational.

I have shown that there is no symmetric predicate in the underlying structure of a transitive copulative verb. Hence some other way must be found to express the fact that this structure is related to the intransitive construction with NP* subject.

NOTES

* This work was supported in part by Grant SLRP-60 from the Council for Research in Applied Psychology. A previous version of this paper appeared as TM-96 of SLRP at TIT. I am indebted to P. R. N. Tic Doulou-reux for discussions which enabled me to deepen my probings. But of course all inadequacies here are my own.

[1] Tic Douloureux pointed out this fact to me.

[2] A closely related structure is that of (i):

(i) Antigone was fucking with Haemon.

There are three arguments that the comitative construction of (i) arises from the NP* construction of (16) through Conjunct-Movement (see Lakoff and Peters, 1966). First, all and only the copulative verbs which have NP* have the comitative. Second, in descriptions of normal heterosexual inter-course, in which the female must be object with such verbs as *screw* and *fuck* in the transitive construction, in the comitative construction she may be subject. This is because in the underlying NP* the fuckers may come in either order, and the first is left as the subject. Finally, if there is an instrument specified, its use must be shared equally by both participants when they are in either intransitive construction, but in the transitive it is used only by the subject:

(ii)   Iphigenia and Electra were using Orestes' tire-pressure gauge to fuck.

(iii) Achilles was using his thumb to fuck Patroclus up the ass.

(iv)   *Orpheus was using a ripped-off gearshift lever to fuck with Eurydice.

[3] This observation I owe to Tic Douloureux.

REFERENCES

Lakoff, George and Stanley Peters. (1966) Phrasal conjunction and symmetric predicates. In D. A. Reibel and S. A. Shane (eds.), *Modern Studies in English*. Englewood Cliffs, N.J.: Prentice-Hall, Inc. 1969.

Quang Phuc Dong. (1968) A note on conjoined noun phrases. In *Quarterly Progress Report* No. 47. South Hanoi: RLET of SHIT (South Hanoi Institute of Technology).

A NOTE ON ONE'S PRIVATES*

P.R.N. TIC DOULOUREUX
Ministere de l'Education de
la Republique Democratique Engadinoise

Contemporary workers in the seminal area of 'generative semantics have been more than happy to confess, with the characteristic modesty of linguists, to the occasional problems encountered in their work: to take the bitter with the sweet; to bite, as it were, the big weenie of failure and seek nourishment therein. To turn momentary setbacks into epochal advances has been their constant creed. A case in point is the recent discovery of Postal (1969) that the abstract representations posited in the theory did less work, perhaps, than might have been anticipated, due to the fact that the components of such representations are inaccessible to syntactic processes operating "outside the word". Postal observed that in a sentence like (1) below, the representation of the subject NP

> (1) An orphan threw a rock through a window.

(an) orphan by a simple word 'orphan' is hopelessly inadequate; clearly, the representation must be closer to that which also underlies 'a child deprived by death of one or usually both parents'. Further research into items like 'child', 'deprive', 'usually', 'parents', etc. will doubtless lead to the discovery of even more oil (or at least natural gas) in this "simple" word, but even this obviously inadequate phrasal representation is an obvious improvement. Yet how are we to account for the fact that the elements of this phrase, though undeniably present in sentence (1), are unable to serve, e.g., as antecedents in the non-process of pronominalization? How, that is, are we to account for the non-occurrence of sentence (2) in the intended reading, in which they refers to the (alas, deceased) parents?

> (2) *An orphan threw a rock through a window because they hadn't had time to teach him not to.

The intended reading is clearly possible for sentence (3):

> (3) A child deprived by death of one or usually both parents threw a rock through a window because they hadn't had time to teach him not to.

The absence of (2) would appear to constitute a severe setback for the proponents of generative semantics. But in the work cited above, Postal (with characteristic boldness) takes the giant step of seizing upon this apparent check as an opportunity for an audacious new theoretical refinement: he develops the concept of the "anaphoric island", according to which all of the material in a phrase marker which is going to become a single word is regarded as delimited universally in such a way as to prevent its influencing anything else. In other words, it's all there; you just can't look at it. That's why you don't see it. The emperor's tailors come to mind as the only suitable precedent for such integrity and insight.

45

This note aims to refine further Postal's insightful notion of the anaphoric island by pointing to a small class of apparent counter-examples. Consider, for example, (4) below:

(4) Someone must have farted; I can smell it.

In this sentence, *it* clearly refers to the gas produced in the hypothetical act of farting; i.e., to the fart itself whose provenance is in question. Hence, we might choose to represent the verb 'to fart' by an expression such as 'to give vent to a fart', and then permit our non-rule of pronominalization to have access to this embedded *fart*. A refinement of the principle of anaphoric islands which would permit just this move has been advanced, in fact, in a recent unwritten work by Ross. He notes a contrast in acceptability between (5a) and (5b):

(5) a. John is a flute-player who likes big ones.
    b. ??John is a flautist who likes big ones.

Ones in both cases is intended to refer to *flutes* ; the difference between (5a) and (5b) is attributed by Ross to the overt appearance of the word *flute(-player)* in (5a) but not (5b).

Ross' proposal, then, is that anaphoric islands are endowed with selective tariffs, which are much less harsh on processes attempting to export parts of the island which are homophonous with its superficial name (or at least with a significant portion thereof) than on processes attempting to export other, non-homophonous parts: a sort of fair labelling practices act. Since the sub-part *flute* of the readings of both *flute-player* and *flautist* is homophonous with a subpart of only the former, it is only from this former NP that its export is permitted, and the contrast between (5a) and (5b) is accounted for.

With this further theoretical advance in hand, we can again approach sentence (4), and find an explanation for the use of *it* in this instance, assuming the representation of the verb 'to fart' suggested above: this contains an NP *fart* which is homophonous with the (whole) surface verb, and is therefore exportable under Ross' principle in the form of an anaphoric relation. Similar examples explicable on the same lines are found in (6), though with decreasing plausibility for the denominal derivation of their included verbs:

(6) a. If you have to shit in here, try not to get it on the rug.
    b. When the gentleman pissed, he got some of it on his foot.
    c. Don't spit into the wind, or it will blow back in your face.
    d. The bowl is there so that when somebody has to puke you can catch it in it.

Regrettably, such explanation breaks down for the following:

(7) a. John bled so much it soaked through his bandage and stained his shirt.
    b. The baby must have diarrhea again; it's running out the side of his diaper and down his leg.
    c. I knew I'd begun to menstruate when I felt it dripping down my thighs.

   d. When Little Johnny threw up, was there any pencil-eraser
       in it?

Though (7a) has a plausible denominal source, *bleed* is not homophonous
with *blood*; (7b) probably involves a derivation from the wrong nouns, since
it in this case refers not to diarrhea but to feces; whatever the precise
sense of *it* in (7c), it is not clear that this item should even be present
in the reading of *menstruate*; and there is no plausible source satisfying
Ross' constraint for (7d). It is apparent that some other principle will
be required to explain these sentences.

     It will be noted immediately that the verbs in question here all
have readings which involve (at least arguably) the mention of the substance which is later referred to anaphorically; thus, although 'to throw
up' is not derived directly from, e.g., an underlying 'to make or produce
throw-up' it does involve something like 'an act or instance of disgorging
the contents of the stomach through the mouth', which contains an approximately suitable NP. Indeed, in this case it is not necessary that the
object of 'throw up' incorporate (in the sense of Gruber) its object NP;
'to throw up one's lunch' is perfectly possible. Many of these verbs, then,
could be regarded as involving the incorporation (optionally or obligatorily, depending on the verb) of the object NP designated for them in their
lexical entries. It would then be these specified NP's which are the antecedents of the *its* in sentences (7). But this principle, too, is much
too broad; deleted designated NPs are not generally eligible to serve as
the antecedents of pronouns, as shown by the sentences in (8):

   (8) a. *When the cannon fired, it hit the ship [where *it* = the
               cannon ball, not the cannon].
       b. *John was eating when I came in, but he did not like its
               taste.
       c. *You can paint the wall, unless it's blue [where *it* = the
               paint you use].
       d. *Harry hasn't been able to fuck since it was cut off by
               the pirates [cf. Wang, 1970, for the incorporation of
               the instrument phrase 'with a penis' in verbs of this
               type].

It is interesting to note that the object implicated in these processes
are available for use in definitization, as pointed out by Karttunen; compare (9) with (8):

   (9) a. When the cannot fired, the ball hit the ship.
       b. John doesn't eat there anymore, because he doesn't like
               the taste of the food.
       c. I want to paint the wall, but I can't find the paint.
       d. Mary let Harry fuck her because she liked the size of
               the prick.

     One might hypothesize, then, that the deleted object of a verb can
be used as the antecedent of a pronoun if the verb is one which represents
a process of expression, ejection, secretion, etc. of some precious bodily
fluid or semi-solid. Other items in this class include *sweat, drool, wipe
one's ass, pick one's nose, lactate, fester, suppurate,* etc.

Even this qualification, however, is not quite narrow enough; the sentences in (10) are appreciably worse than those in (4), (6) and (7):

(10) a. ??Mary was crying on my shoulder again last night; she got it all over my new jacket.
   b. ??John is still breathing, but it's bad [where *it* = John's breath].

It in (10a) is intended to refer to Mary's tears (if it be objected that *tears* is a count noun, let the reader substitute *them* for *it*); the anomaly resides in the feeling that some snide and sordid comment is being made about the substance Mary exudes on my shoulder. Apparently, then, we need to restrict the process not simply to body products, but to the sort of body products one doesn't generally go about exuding in public.

The principle given above deals with the examples given so far: anaphora is possible when the antecedent is an unmentionable substance serving as a designated object in an anaphoric island. Presumably, the islands are delighted to export such substances. There are, however, yet other examples, where the substance in question does not seem to be present in the reading at all, but is simply implied by what is present there:

(11) a. I guess my wife has been balling the postman again, because they've gotten it all over the sheets.
   b. If you're going to masturbate, you should go in the bathroom where it'll be easier to clean it up.
   c. Mary tried to give John a blow job, but she choked on it [ambiguous, depending on Mary's success].

Verbs like *ball*, *masturbate*, *give someone a blow job*, etc. do not essentially involve ejaculation (the presumable deleted object of which is the antecedent of the pronouns in (11)), as will be attested by the devotees of certain strange means of birth control, pre-pubescent boys, certain *castrati*, etc.; in any case, even if it occurs (indeed, even if it usually occurs), it is in an important sense not part of the essence of what is going on, and as such not a part of the meaning or assertion of the sentence, but rather a part of what is (perhaps for inductive reasons) inferrable from it.

We arrive, accordingly, at a principle of English grammar which does not, in fact, violate Postal's important constraint on export from anaphoric islands: Whenever a sentence has a semantic interpretation making reference to an action or event that (inferentially) results in the production of an unmentionable bodily substance, such a substance can be referred to by a pronoun *it* within the sentence, and indeed an otherwise antecedentless *it* in such a disgusting environment usually takes such an interpretation. This principle is probably related to that which establishes the referents of definites in sentences like (9), or of NPs like *the sun* and *the moon* (for terrestrial speakers) and *the dog* or *the baby* (in domestic contexts) from implicatures and factual knowledge of the situation rather than from syntactically definable relations like those involved in ordinary definitization and non-pronominalization. Perhaps one could call these world-creating verbs,with Lakoff; 'world-defiling' might be a better term. The principle is also sure to be related to the type of ostentatious taboo displayed by sentences like (12):

(12) a. Look at them! They're doing it in the road!
     b. Mommy, baby made a you-know-what on the oriental!

Having now isolated the phenomenon, we can raise the issue of its distribution in the languages of the world. In fact, sentences illustrating the same process can be found elsewhere among the Indo-European languages:[1]

(13) (Latin) Servi, ancillae, si quis eorum sub centone crepuit, quod ego non sensi, nullum mihi vitium facit.
                                  -Cato the elder
     'Servants, handmaidens, if any one of them farteth under his toga, and I do not smell it, it makes no difference to me.'

(14) (Hittite) ...DUMU.É.[(GA)]L šu-up-pí ụa-a-tar pa-ra-a e-epi-zi [(LUGAL)]-ị SAL-LUGAL-ịa LUGAL-uš III-ŠU a-i-iš-še-et a-ar-ri [(ta-at)] ḫụ-ụr-ti-ịa-[(li)]-ịa la-a-ḫu-i SAL.LUGAL-sa III-SU u-i-is-se-et
     [(a-a)]r-ri na-at ḫu-ur-ti-ịa-li-ịa la-a-hu i
                               -KBoXVII vs. 1 14-17
     'The equerry proffers pure water to the king and the queen. The king washes his mouth three times and spits it [=the used water] into the basin. The queen also washes her mouth three times and spits it into the basin.'

As any self-respecting comparativist knows, the establishment of a phenomenon in three branches of a language family (in this case, Germanic, Italic and Anatolian) furnishes a secure basis for attributing it to the proto-language. Thus, we are justified in placing the type of anaphoric non-process under consideration at least within common Indo-European.

We can also, however, observe similar facts in other language families. Consider the following Turkish sentences:[2]

(15) a. Kedi yere işedi; onu temizler misin?
       'The cat pissed on the floor; will you clean it up?'
                               [(cf. (15b)]
     b. Hasan çişi temizledi.
       'Hasan cleaned up the piss.' [note the non-homophony of çişi here with işedi in (15a)]
     c. Bebek yere kustu; onu temizler misin?
       'The baby threw up on the floor; will you clean it up?'

Similar to (15a), we find sentence (16) in Finnish:

(16) Kissa oksensi lattialle, ja minä pyyhin sen pois.
     'Cat   barfed on floor and I   wipe   it away.'

In neither the Turkish (15a) nor the Finnish (16) does the verb have a corresponding homophonous noun representing the product of the act; comparison of (15a) and (15b) establishes this for Turkish, while the only noun directly derivable from the stem of Finnish *oksensi* has the sense 'act of barfing'. When we observe sentences of the same type in Hungarian (cf. (17)), we can conclude that this phenomenon can be attributed to proto-Ural-Altaic, assuming the unity of this family:

> (17) Aladár becsinált, és most hordja magaval.
> 'Aladar crapped in his pants, and now he is carrying it around with him.'

Sentences like (18) in Japanese might then be cited as further evidence for the affinity of this language with Ural-Altaic, a connection that has sometimes been hypothesized:

> (18) Akanbo ga tatami no ue ni haite simaimasita. Sono naka
> ni ti ga mazzite-imasu.
> 'The baby wound up throwing up on the floor-mat. There is some blood mixed in with it.'

At this point, however, the credibility of even the most imperialistic of comparativists strains. An Indo-European-Ural-Altaic linguistic unity is indeed possible, in which case the syntactic non-process which concerns us here must be one of its most archaic features, but a non-genetic account might be preferred.

The alternative, of course, is to claim that we have here to do with a universal. Such a move would be entirely natural, given the climate of opinion resulting from the imaginative researches of Postal, but this hypothesis is rather harder to check than some, given the general reluctance of informants to give away fundamental cultural secrets of the sort required for the construction of the relevant examples. We are told[3] that such sentences do not occur in Chinese or the Algonquian languages, but given the general paucity of anaphoric processes involving ellipsis in these languages, this is perhaps to be expected. Sentence (19), however, seems to furnish conclusive proof. It is from Mam, a Mayan language spoken in Huehuetenango Province, Guatemala:[4]

> (19) Ma-∅-kub?-n-ča:?-n-e. Ma-∅-či?-t-šo?-n Tat Wan t-e: Tat Čep.
> 'Earlier today I crapped downward, and Senor John threw it at Senor Peter.'

Mayan affinities with the other languages cited above being rather questionable, it seems plausible to assert that the process of euphemistic anaphora is a universal aspect of pronominalization non-processes. The possibility of borrowing (in this case, from Spanish) cannot be completely neglected, of course, but let's try.

As is well known, once we have shown something to be universal we no longer have to explain it. Accordingly, the overall inconclusiveness of these remarks is just what is to be expected. By demostrating euphemism to be a general property of anaphora, we have made it possible to maintain Postal's momentous insights. The tapeworm of universality, as it were, has purged us of another apparently embarrassing particularity, and Science marches on. In the process of explicating the non-diffi-culties posed by the above facts, we hope incidentally to have made some modest contribution to linguistic theory, in the form of the first known filthy-substantive universal of language.

NOTES

* No one who supported this work had better find out about it.

[1] These facts were pointed out to me by Prof. Muhammad Gumbal of the Tbilisi Institute of Tagmemics.

[2] These facts make me indebted to Dr. It Dik of the Ankara Semantics Society and the Fellowship for the Advancement of Generative Semantics.

[3] By the eminent polyglot Dr. Snively Bugger, Oxon.

[4] This sentence was provided us in return for a bottle of Ripple by an Indian who called himself Ča-če?w. Some failure of communication is perhaps to be suspected, as this means Horseshit in Mam.

REFERENCES

Postal, Paul M. (1969) Anaphoric islands. To appear in *Linguistic Inquiry*.

Wang, Munç. (1970) Copulative sentences in English, a Gmc. language of Northern Deleware.

ON ABSTRACT DRECATIVE NOUNS[*]

NOAH A. TWADDLE
Commonwealth Institute of Agronomy

and

COUGHLAKE SWEAT
State Teacher's College at Moot Point

The prepositional phrase *into* + NP co-occurs not only with motion verbs (*run into the house*), inchoative and passive verbs (*get into trouble*; *change into a werewolf*), and certain other verbs whose classification is as yet unclear, such as *change* in the sense of *change one's clothes* (*change into a new suit*), but also (very often in the reduced form *in* + NP) with a class of verbs which we call "drecatives", and which includes not only the old familiar ****, ****, ****, ****, and ****, but also ****, ** (both of which are usually motion verbs or inchoatives: *Harry went crazy*; *Sam came to be obnoxious*), **** (usually a causative or creation verb: *make a chair*; *make her leave*), and many other verbs not usually placed in this class, such as *retch, belch, slabber, cough, bleed*, and the like. Various other properties show that this is indeed a coherent class of verbs and not just a bunch of unrelated words accidentally sharing a syntactic property.

In this paper we propose that each of these verbs is derived from an underlying structure containing an abstract drecative noun, which, if it ever appears overtly in surface structure at all, is clearly felt to be redundant. Thus sentence (1), containing the verb ****, we will argue, is derived from a deep structure[1] something like that in Diagram 1. The details of this diagram we do not consider important; in all likelihood this tree structure is far too simplified.[2] The crucial point is that the deep structure contains the abstract drecative noun ****.

(1) Harry was so scared that he **** in his pants.

We have accumulated thirty-nine arguments for this proposal, but will only present a few here.[3]

1. Consider sentences (2) and (3).

(2) Harry ****s.
(3) Harry ****ed.

Notice that although there is no overt object, it is clear that (2) is usually interpreted as (4) and (3) is usually interpreted as (5). This could not be explained unless, in fact, (2) and (4) are derived from the same deep structure and (3) and (5) too share a common deep structure.[4]

(4) Harry ****s ****.
(5) Harry ****ed ****.

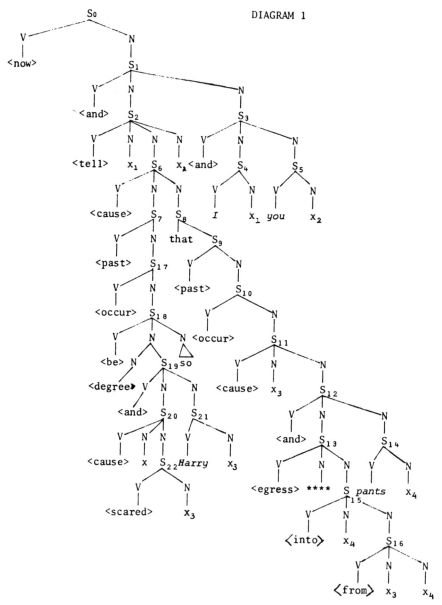

DIAGRAM 1

2. The second argument involves the passive. Although sentences like (6) superficially appear to contain transitive verb phrases, in fact it is easy to show that the supposed object of the verb is a complement, since such sentences do not passivize. Cf. (7).

(6) Harry blew his nose into his handkerchief.

(7) *His nose was blown by Harry into his handkerchief.

Furthermore, *blow one's nose* is transparently a lexical unit like ****,
**** or ****; thus the inability of supposedly transitive verb phrases
like *blow one's nose* and *move one's bowels* to passivize is explained by
the supposed object actually being part of the verb. This in turn supports,
at least impressionistically (that is, by means of our native speaker's
Sprachahnungen), the claim that the drecative verbs, such as ****, ****,
and *eructate*, contain an underlying drecative noun.

    3. Consider now the sentences in (8).

      (8) a. Harry blew his nose and then he ate it.
         b. Harry puked and had to wipe it up.

Whay does *it* refer to in (8)? Most speakers would interpret *it* in (8a) as
referring not to the supposed object of *blow*, namely *his nose*, but rather
to what we will propose as a covert, abstract, drecative, namely **** .
Similarly, in (8b), although *puke* has no overt object, the *it* must refer
to the incorporated drecative noun **** (Perhaps, better, <puke>). Without this assumption, there is no way of explaining the reference of the *it*.

    4. There are two scope arguments that show that *almost* in sentences
like those in (9) where there is overtly only one predicate per sentence, is
ambiguous in scope and can modify either of two underlying predicates.

      (9) a. Sam almost ran into the house.
         b. Bill almost barfed into the sink.
         c. Igor almost bled all over his shirt.

The adverb occuring in these sentences cannot be preposed to the front of
the sentence in most, but not all, English dialects (cf. (10).

      (10) a. *Into the house, Sam ran.
         b. *Into the sink, Bill barfed.
         c. *All over his shirt, Igor bled.

However, the adverb can be topicalized, at least marginally:

      (11) a. ?It was into the house that Sam ran.
         b. ?It was into the sink that Bill barfed.
         c. ?It was all over his shirt that Igor bled.

What this suggests is that the relevant restriction is not an adverb-pre-
posing restriction, but rather an adverb-movement restriction; specifically,
it is a restriction on adverb-movement out of a complement sentence. Cf.
(12b) from (12a).

      (12) a. Sam told them to leave tomorrow.
         b. *Tomorrow, Sam told them to leave.

For the same reason that all but a few select dialects do not allow (12b),
they do not allow (10).[5]

    The second argument, similar to one devised by Morgan le Faye for *kill*, supports this hypothesis. (13a) is ambiguous, as shown by the possible continuations (13b) and (13c).

(13) a. Harry almost blew his nose....
  b. ....but nothing happened when he tried.
  c. ....but he was stopped.
  d. Harry blew his nose.

That is, in the (b) reading of (13a), Harry tried to blow his nose but nothing happened; in the (c) reading he was prevented from even trying. The only possible difference is in what part of (13d) is modified by *almost* in (13a). In the (c) reading of (13a) it modifies the entire (13d), but in the (b) sense it modifies some verb which itself is within the predicate in the underlying structure, and likely one which is itself within the scope of the outermost predicate.

  This suggests that since we are dealing with motive adverbials, there is in the deep structure a motive verb, and that part of the underlying structure of a sentence like (9b) is precisely a phrase consisting of an abstract drecative noun as subject, an abstract motive verb, <go>, as the predicate, and the overt adverbial of the surface structure, as in Diagram 2.

....   DIAGRAM 2

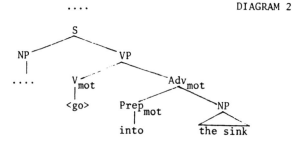

(9) b. Bill barfed into the sink.

  5. The adverbs which co-occur with these verbs are totally inexplicable if we do not assume some underlying structure such as that in Diagrams 1 and 2. Consider (14) and (15).

(14) a. Pawkins ****ed 3 feet.
  b. Pawkins ****ed in an arc.
  c. Pawkins ****ed around the corner.
  d. Pawkins ****ed through a tissue.

(15) a. Gulliver ****ed blue.
  b. Gulliver ****ed his name in the snow.
  c. Gulliver ****ed the fire out at the royal palace.

An adverbial of length such as *3 feet* can only be a locative measure adverbial as with verbs of measure (16) or a motive adverbial with a verb of motion as in (17).

(16) a. The patio extends 3 feet.
     b. The desktop measures 3 feet.

(17) a. Pawkins ran 3 feet.
     b. Pawkins jumped 3 feet.

But in (14a) there is neither a verb of measure nor (overtly) a verb of motion, although here *3 feet* is clearly a motive adverbial. Therefore we can only explain its presence by an underlying verb of motion. But Pawkins in (16a) cannot be the subject of such a verb of motion since he could very well have ****ed without moving from place. Therefore the subject of this underlying verb of motion is also a non-overt noun.

Similarly, the adverbs in (14b-d) can only be locative or "Gestalt" (as in (18)) or motive (as in (19)).

(18) a. Pawkins bent in an arc.
     b. The lines joined in an arc.
     c. Tom spent all that time around the corner.
     d. To show the cohesion of wet paper, he kept his finger through a wet tissue.

(19) a. Pawkins threw the ball in an arc.
     b. Pawkins threw the ball around the corner.
     c. Pawkins chased the thief around the corner.
     d. Pawkins poked his finger through a tissue.

Again, the only explanation possible is that the adverbs of (14) are motive. Indeed, the commonest type of adverbial occurring with drecative verbs are those, like those in (14), that are usually locative-motive.

But other types of adverbials also occur with drecative verbs, as shown in (15), though these also support the analysis. What can *blue* in (15a) mean? With a causative (as in (20)) it is clear what *blue* means as an adverb, as it is when it is the complement of a verb of judgement (21).

(20) a. I painted the house blue.
     b. Gainsborough colored the boy blue.

(21) a. I thought the picture blue (but it was actually blue-green).
     b. I'd prefer the walls blue (but I'd settle for them being green).

But *blue* in (15a) cannot be the type of adverb it is in either (20) or (21) since **** is neither a causative nor a complement verb. *Blue* in (15a) refers to what is being ****ed, but there is no overt object in the sentence.

Even the (15b) sentences can provide an argument. Although it is true that formally the overt subject and verb are enough to account for the complements, semantically they are not enough to do so. For example, it would not be enough for Gulliver to have merely ****ed in order to mark his name in the snow or to have put a fire out. As we know from reading Swift, he must **** on the snow in the place where the letters will be to form them, and he must **** on the royal palace in the place where the fire is, the **** itself snuffing out the flames. Therefore the directed motion of a fluid must be referred to in an account of the semantics of (15b).

6. Let us turn now to a non-drecative verb but one closely related to them: *empty*, an inchoative meaning 'become empty' or 'come to be empty', or a causative meaning 'cause to empty', 'cause to become empty', 'cause to come to be empty'. Presumably, the underlying structure of a sentence like (22) is something like that in Diagram 3.

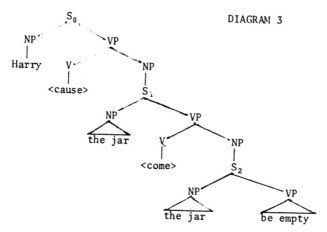

DIAGRAM 3

(22) Harry emptied the jar.

Considering (23), where can the adverb be assigned in Diagram 3? What does it modify?

(23) a. Harry emptied the jar into the pool.
b. Harry emptied his bladder into the urinal.

To begin with, we are again confronted with motive verbs; if there are underlying verbs of motion in (23a) and (23b), their respective subjects cannot be the overt nominals *the jar* or *his bladder*, since in (23a) it is not the jar that goes into the pool, but what was within the jar; in (23b) it is not the bladder that goes into the urinal, but what was in the bladder. The emptying in each case consists precisely of removing what was within them into, respectively, the pool and the urinal. Reconstructing the lowest S of Diagram 3 on this basis we get (for (23b)), Diagram 4.

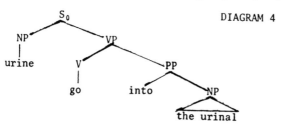

DIAGRAM 4

Now compare (24) and (6):

> (24) Harry emptied his nose into his handkerchief.

> (6) Harry blew his nose into his handkerchief.

The only difference between these is that while in (24) it is (pragmatically?) implied that Harry cleared his nose by blowing it, in (6) it is explicitly stated that he did so. The only difference between the deep structure of the two, accordingly, should be an additional adverbial in that of (6).

SUMMARY

We have presented a half dozen arguments for drecative verbs being derived transformationally from underlying deep structures containing verbs of motion whose subjects are abstract drecative nouns. A great many problems in connection with this analysis remain, but we feel that the evidence is quite conclusive and provides yet another example of how the overt surface form of a sentence may be considerably different from and contain wildly different sets of lexical items from its covert, underlying form.

APPENDIX: Drecative and other verbs

I.		II.		III.		IV.	
	vomit		expectorate		slobber		****
	spew		****		slabber		break wind
	****		**** up		slaver		
	retch		belch		drool	V.	go
	barf		belch out				****
	bring up		eruct				make
			eructate				eliminate
							defecate
							void

VI.		VII.		VIII.		IX.	
	****		sneeze		breathe		perspire
	leak				exhale		sweat
	urinate				blow		ooze
X.	bleed	XI.	come (off)		cough		drain
			ejaculate	X.	evacuate		excrete
					empty		drip
					clear		

ADDENDUM

While bugging a few rooms and phonelines, we recently overheard a conversation between Morgan le Faye, the Green Knight, and Lancelot of Benwick. Apparently sentences like those in (8) may not provide as good an argument as we had thought, since you also get sentences like *Tom and Sue were making it on the sofa and when they came they had a lot of trouble cleaning it up.* Since the microphone was of poor quality, we were not sure of this example; in any case it does not impress us as a counterexample.

However, the example *Harry chopped off Sue's head and had to clean it up*, referring to the attendant mess, does. There were several other bad (for our proposals) cases, but we are saving those for a review of Roman de Clef's forthcoming book, *Le franglais vivant*, Gallimard, to appear, 1972.

NOTES

* This paper consists of an analysis of sentences surreptitiously written down by us while overhearing conversations between Q. P. Dong, the Green Knight, Morgan le Faye, and Lancelot of Benwick. We claim as our modest achievement only the analysis, for we are too clean-minded ever to have thought up examples like the ones we have stolen. The authors would like to thank Miss Hermione Dimwitty for her helpful remarks and criticisms; she will see that we have published the paper anyway.

[1] Rabid generative semanticists may read "semantic representation".

[2] In keeping with standard scientific practice, what we don't at all understand we carefully disregard.

[3] The argument based on the fact that you can't say sentence (i) we are saving for a forthcoming article 'Abstract drecative nouns in English', to appear in *Papers in Linguistics*, volume 18 (1972). The rest we are saving to read at a couple of future conferences.

(i) *Harry blew Shirley's nose into his (or her) handkerchief.

[4] It is true that (2) could marginally be interpreted as, for example, (ii), and (3) likewise as (iii), but this does not affect the argument here.

(ii) Harry ****s $\left\{ \begin{array}{l} \text{bile.} \\ \text{blood.} \\ \text{....} \end{array} \right\}$

(iii) Harry ****ed $\left\{ \begin{array}{l} \text{bile.} \\ \text{blood.} \\ \text{....} \end{array} \right\}$

[5] Although (v) is a good transform of (iv), (vi) is not. Therefore (iv) must be ambiguous; in one reading *in Jane's mouth* is a "motive" adverb, in the other locative.

(iv) Harry **** in Jane's mouth.
(v) In Jane's mouth, Harry ****.
(vi) *In Jane's mouth Harry ****.

ON FUCKING (WELL)
A STUDY OF SOME QUASI-PERFORMATIVE EXPRESSIONS

TINA BOPP (Mrs. Franz)
Donnybrook College

In this paper evidence will be presented for treating as members of the same lexical class the words *fucking*, *bloody* and *shitting*, and for considering these to have the predictable variants (in some dialects) *fucking well*, *bloody well*, and *shitting well*.[1][2] Examples of this class are:

(1) a.
You $\left\{ \begin{array}{l} \text{fucking (well)} \\ \text{bloody (well)} \\ \text{?shitting} \end{array} \right\}$ took your time.

b.
$\left\{ \begin{array}{l} \text{Fucking (well)} \\ \text{Bloody (well)} \\ \text{?Shitting} \end{array} \right\}$ make up your mind.

(2) a.
Turn off that $\left\{ \begin{array}{l} \text{fucking} \\ \text{bloody} \\ \text{shitting} \end{array} \right\}$ radio.

b.
$\left\{ \begin{array}{l} \text{Some} \\ \text{The} \end{array} \right\} \left\{ \begin{array}{l} \text{fucking} \\ \text{bloody} \\ \text{?shitting} \end{array} \right\}$ idiot left the top off the brandy bottle.

c. Bloody idiots, forgetting the blasting caps.
d. Fucking sons of bitches, they wrecked my car.
e. Shitting cats, always yowling all night.

These expressions have been demonstrated to be related to the 'quasi-verbs' rather than the real verbs *shit* and *fuck* (Quang, 1969:49ff., esp. note 9). The real verbs *shit* and *fuck* will henceforth be designated $shit_v$ and $fuck_v$ as opposed to $shit_q$ and $fuck_q$. There are no relative clauses containing either $shit_v$ or $fuck_v$, nor $shit_q$ and $fuck_q$,[3] and furthermore none with *bloody* as predicate adjective,[4] corresponding to (2).

(3)
*Turn off that radio which is $\left\{ \begin{array}{l} \text{fucking.} \\ \text{shitting.} \\ \text{bloody.} \end{array} \right\}$

(4)
*Turn off that radio which $\left\{ \begin{array}{l} \text{fuck.} \\ \text{shit on.} \end{array} \right\}$

To continue the possible tests for determining the syntactic properties of *fucking*, *bloody* and *shitting*, which one would superficially want to compare with adjectives, we note that Ross (1969) demonstrates that (non-stative) adjectives behave like NPs in undergoing pseudoclefting:

> (5) a. What John did was be obnoxious.
>   b.*What John did was be tall.

But such sentences are not possible with the class of words under discussion:

> (6) *What the idiot did was be fucking
>   shitting
>   bloody

> (7) *What the radio was was fucking
>   shitting
>   bloody

Likewise *fucking well*, *shitting well* and *bloody well*, as in (1), are superficially similar to adverbs. But most adverbs, other than those like *very*, *extremely* etc. and directional adverbs, can be preposed.

> (8) Quietly
>   Deftly
>   With a curious tool   , John picked the lock.
>   For King and country

> (9) *Fucking
>   *Bloody   (well), you took your time.
>   *Shitting

Adverbials not in the verb phrase can be contrasted, and the second occurrence of VP in conjoined sentences can be pronominalized by *do so*.

> (10) John left quickly and Ferd did so quietly.

> (11) a. *John fucking well paid up and you'd better do so bloody
>   well.
>   b. John fucking well paid up and you'd bloody well better
>   do so.
>   c. John fucking well paid up and I advise you to bloody well
>   do so.   fucking well

The preposing test and the *do so* test thus yield conflicting results, except when *fucking* etc. are stressed and/or follow *do so*. Note that in (11b) and (11c), *fucking* and *bloody well* are unstressed; the lack of stress on the second occurrence of a member of our hypothetical class may indicate that each of the members has approximately the same meaning or equivalent meaning. This question will be discussed somewhat later in this paper. We will conclude that *fucking* etc. are syntactically unlike the usual types of adjective and adverb, though there are some similarities to be explored shortly, and on the principle established by Quang, we will call them quasi-adjectives and adverbs. It still remains for us, of course, to establish (1) their meaning and (2) the syntactic and other constraints on their use.

Leaving aside the question of meaning for the moment, there are a number of interesting syntactic properties to be noted. Reflexes of

$fuck_q$ and $shit$ on_q turn up as surface quasi-adverbs, quasi-adjectives and nouns.[5] *Fucking* behaves very much like *bloody*, and turns up in the prenominal positions occupied by adjectives:

(10) I'm a fucking artist, I'm not a fucking P.R. agent.[6]
(John Lennon, *Rolling Stone* 1-21-1971,p.41)

For some speakers, including Lennon, who may not count here because he speaks a dialect of British English, *fucking* is also possible with verbs[7] and some adverbs.

(11) I'm not technically good, but I can make it fucking howl and move. (ibid, p.35)
(12) Everybody was probably thinking they're not going to fucking work on it. (ibid, p.47)
(13) He fucking went home instead of waiting.
(14) He can't fucking (well) make it today.
(15) He fucking (well) can't make it today.
(16) I'm not going to wait fucking (well) forever.

In the most liberal dialects, the quasi-adjective *fucking* seems to go with any sort of noun, and the number of occurrences in a sentence is not necessarily restricted to one.

(17) Fucking sincerity will get you nowhere. (abstract noun)
(18) He was full of fucking arsenic.   (mass noun)
(19) The fucking cats are under the fucking bed. (count nouns)
(20) (That) fucking Charley refuses to admit he works for the CIA.
(21) Who did you expect, the fucking Three Musketeers?[8]

The position of *fucking* after the article and number sometimes indicates a difference of emphasis and meaning. For some speakers the following are synonymous:

(22) Hamlet is a fucking hard part to play.
(23) Hamlet is a hard fucking part to play.

Others distinguish a meaning in which *fucking* emphasizes *hard*

(24) That part is fucking hard to play. (as in (22))

from the meaning which associates *fucking* with the whole NP or perhaps just *part*, as in

(25) It's hard to play that fucking part right.

Similar distinctions are, I think, to be found in the use of the adverbial *fucking* (*well*). I find it hard to find separate meanings for

(26) Shut the door and fucking (well) do it quietly.
(27) Shut the door and do it fucking (well) quietly.
(28) Fucking well take out the trash now.
(29) Take out the trash fucking well now.

because of the fact that sentences like the above can have a reading in which the adverbial is asserted (cf. Lakoff 1970, Jackendoff lecture 1968). It is hard for me to assign different readings to (26)-(29) in which the disapproval of the whole proposition is distinct from disapproval associated with the adverbial. But with more than one adverbial, some differences do emerge.

(30) Fucking (well) empty the trash now in the backyard quietly.
(31) Empty the trash fucking (well) now, in the backyard, quietly.
(32) Empty the trash now in the fucking backyard, quietly.
(33) Empty the trash now in the backyard fucking well quietly.

The appearance of *fucking*, and not *fucking well*, in (32) brings up the point of how the syntactic category, or quasi-category, of $fuck_q$ is determined. Adverbials consisting of a preposition and NP allow only the quasi-adjective form:

(34) a. The skunk fucking well was in the backyard
     b. The skunk was fucking well in the backyard.
(35) *Those woodchucks were eating the beams fucking well in the basement.
(36) Those woodchucks were eating the beams in the fucking basement.
(37) Do it fucking well discreetly.
(38) Do it with (some) fucking discretion.

These facts of course concern only those idiolects which distinguish between *fucking*, *bloody* and *fucking well*, *bloody well*..

I have claimed that *fucking well* does not precede preposition + NP combinations, and that in these cases *fucking* precedes the NP. This is not the case in (39) and (40), and in just those cases where the NP is pronominal, either unstressed and anaphoric, or contrastively stressed:

(39) He can't blow up the Empire State Building singlehandedly
     so I'll have to $\left\{ \begin{array}{l} \text{fucking well go with him.} \\ \text{go fucking well with him.} \\ \text{*go with fucking him.} \end{array} \right\}$

(40) Charley was mad
     when I told him I wouldn't $\left\{ \begin{array}{l} \text{fucking well go with him.} \\ \text{*go with fucking him.} \\ \text{?*go fucking well with him.} \end{array} \right\}$

Although (41) is grammatical, in general *fucking* can't precede a low or unstressed NP:

(41) Go with $\left\{ \begin{array}{l} \text{the fucking bastard.} \\ \text{*fucking him.} \end{array} \right\}$

(42) Fucking well go with $\left\{ \begin{array}{l} \text{the bastard.} \\ \text{him.} \end{array} \right\}$

(43) Go fucking well with $\left\{ \begin{array}{l} \text{the bastard.} \\ \text{him.} \end{array} \right\}$

Bastard has some stress in (41) though it is used anaphorically, and *him* in (40) is contrastively stressed, so restricting *fucking* only to positions before stressed elements does not account for the ungrammaticality of *fucking* and any personal pronoun.

The alternative explanation which immediately suggests itself is that *fucking* is itself part of the NP replaced by the pronoun. In that case, the pronoun *him* refers to *that fucking Charley* in

(43) a. That fucking Charley was mad when I told him I wouldn't
go with $\begin{Bmatrix} \text{him.} \\ \text{him.} \end{Bmatrix}$

b. *That fucking Charley was mad when I told fucking him that I wouldn't go with him.

c. *That fucking Charley was mad when I told him I wouldn't go with fucking him.

But is there any justification for deriving (43a) from (43d) rather than (43e)?

(43) d. That fucking Charley$_i$ was mad when I told that fucking Charley$_i$ that I wouldn't go with that fucking Charley$_i$.

e. That fucking Charley$_i$ was mad when I told Charley$_i$ that I wouldn't go with $\begin{Bmatrix} \text{Charley}_i \\ \text{emph.Charley} \end{Bmatrix}$.

It seems to me that it is a matter of choice on the part of the speaker whether any or all of the tokens of a NP in a sentence has *fucking* etc. associated with it, not a condition that has to be met in order for certain certain NPs to be identical for some purpose. But it is also true that *fucking* etc. never precede any sort of pronoun, which would be true if *fucking* etc., were just a part of the entire NP which was identical in reference to the pronominalized NP. In the absence of clearer facts about the anaphoric identity of NPs in (43) I will simply assume it to be infelicitous for *fucking* to precede a pronominalized NP, of the ordinary sort. Destressed pronominal nouns may be combined with *fucking* quite freely:

(43) f. Charley$_i$ got mad when I told the fucking idiot$_i$ to fuck off.

g. Charley$_i$ got mad when I told the fucking idiot$_j$ to fuck off.

So if one of the constituents happens to be an ordinary anaphoric pronoun, *fucking* can be associated only with the whole proposition or with some unpronominalized constituent, and not with the constituent it is semantically associated with. Thus many semantically possible combinations cannot be said grammatically.

The question which naturally arises is what possible explanation or explanations are to be found in the theory of syntax for the manifestation of something which means 'speaker disapproves of x' where x is a proposition or an NP within a proposition. Of course, 'DISAPPROVES' is not sufficient to characterize the meaning of *fucking* in (10), which contains clauses in which *fucking* is used with two different meanings. I do not think that in (10) Lennon disparages artists, but he does, probably, intend to disparage P.R. agents by contrast. Furthermore, (44) is not contradictory:

(44)

$$\text{On Baile's Strand is a } \begin{Bmatrix} *\text{shitting} \\ \text{fucking} \\ \text{bloody} \end{Bmatrix} \text{great-assed play.}[9]$$

Fucking resembles *bad, wicked, mean* etc., in having a primary pejorative meaning which is altered in some undefinable contexts to mean the opposite: 'great, fine' and so on.

Assuming that all the meanings of *fucking* can, in the best of all possible worlds, be accounted for satisfactorily, there remains the question of whether *fuck, shit on, bloody, damn* and variants *fucking, shitting* have different meanings in their pejorative uses. I myself am inclined to think not. Which one is used seems to me to be just a matter of random choice, a matter of 'euphony' or parallelism, and finally a function of an individual's scale of the shock value which he associates with, for instance, *blasted* vs. *shitting*. I see no semantic difference between (45a) and (45b).

(45) a. The fucking $\begin{Bmatrix} \text{dog} \\ \text{bloody} \end{Bmatrix}$ knocked over the fucking garbage can.[10]

    b. The $\begin{Bmatrix} \text{shitting} \\ \text{damn} \end{Bmatrix}$ dog knocked over the fucking garbage can.

The general meaning of such items is to indicate some sort of disapproval connected with a proposition or a constituent of it. This is part of the meaning of the sentence, and must be represented syntactically. I would like to make the guess that the syntactic structure resembles that of a performative which determines, in this case sometimes in conjunction with another performative, the illocutionary force of an utterance.[11] The performatives which associate some feature with a proposition or a part of one are question and possibly also whatever is responsible for contrastive stress. In both cases some constituent is marked. Like Question and Imperative, *fuck* and *shit on* and *damn* may not appear in restrictive or non-restrictive relative clauses (see note 4). In any case, such an analysis with the performative is in accord with Quang's penetrating observation that *fucking* in (46) is attributed to the speaker of the utterance, not the quoted speaker.

(46) John says that his landlord is a fucking scoutmaster.

I would agree, with the qualification that even if John is being quoted verbatim, the speaker must agree that there is something disagreeable about scoutmasters. DISAPPROVE is compatible with most types of performative (declarative, questions, rude imperatives, promises, etc,). The exception is the polite imperative noted by Lakoff (oral tradition)

(47) Shut the fucking door, $\begin{Bmatrix} \text{will you?} \\ *\text{won't you?} \end{Bmatrix}$

in which the tag question *won't you* indicates an inappropriate sort of politeness or deference.

One final phonological feature should be mentioned. It was mentioned previously that *fucking* etc., cannot precede some constituents with relatively low stress. This is not true just of constituents. It is possible to permute the *fucking* modifying a constituent between certain parts of the constituent which need not themselves be constituents! Most people are familiar with *abso-fucking-lutely*; *abso* and *lutely* are clearly not constituents. But this permutation is possible only if the primary word-stress follows *fucking*.

(48) It's auto-fucking-mátic.
(49) *I ate at the aúto-fucking-mat.
(50) He's a snob because he's diplo-bloody-mátic.
(51) *He's a snob because he's a díplo-bloody-mat.

Compounds with final stress also allow the permutation, and normal initially stressed compounds do not:

(52) He's the vice-fucking-président.
(53) *He doesn't get to live in the White fucking House.
(54) He's the fucking vice-président.

I maintain that (48)-(53) are the result of a permutation rule because I see no difference in meaning between (54) and (52). It seems that just a strong phonological constraint which conspires to produce certain sorts of rhytmic patterns prevents the permutation from applying.

NOTES

An earlier version of this paper was read at the Hallowe'en meeting of the Linguistic Circle of Staten Island under the title ****ing, ****ing and ******. I am grateful to Ei. Adelaide Huhn for calling my attention to interesting corresponding forms in Tocharian and Hittite, which it was, however, beyond the scope of this paper to include. I am grateful also to several friends who provided information and judgments of grammaticality; through no fault of theirs one of them is currently being prosecuted by the telephone company for using the telephone for obscene purposes, because of one of our telephone discussions of the material in this paper.

My debt to the great trailblazers in this field, Quang Phuc Dong and his follower V. S. Anantalingam, is of course obvious.

[1] People I have gotten judgments of grammaticality from seem to have very strong conflicting opinions, perhaps even more so than on the usual sort of syntactic data. The cultural prohibitions against this style of speech may have inhibited some people I consulted. I myself, though a graduate of a girls' college, have only a passive command of this style, but even so, I find I have fairly strong notions of what could be said and what could not.

[2] *shitting (well)* may be considerably more restricted than the others for most speakers. For instance Quang (1969) notes that *shitting* is not freely substitutable for *fucking*, though *shit on* and *fuck* are mutually substitutable.

Other restrictions on *shitting* are of an interesting nature.

     (a) He's a shitting prick.(not used anaphorically)
     (b) He's a fucking ass-hole.

are both grammatical,

     (c) *He's a shitting ass-hole.
     (d) *He's a fucking prick.

are both ungrammatical. I guess this is because of the ambiguity of *fucking* and *shitting* in (c) and (d) with the verbs *fuck* and *shit*, which would seem to refer to the actions of anatomical structures, rather than indicating that an individual, who is either an inept or idiotic person, or someone officious and obnoxious, is disapproved of by the speaker. On the other hand, the existence of a personal pronoun *he* should presuppose that the referent of *prick* and *ass-hole* is human, at least animate.

[3]   Quang (1969, footnote 9)   notes that there is no sentence corresponding to the structure

     (a) Drown that cat$_i$
$$\left\{ \begin{array}{l} \text{Fuck that cat}_i \\ \text{Shit on that cat}_i \end{array} \right\}$$

such as

     (b) Drown that cat which $\left\{ \begin{array}{l} \text{fuck} \\ \text{shit on} \end{array} \right\}$

It should be noted that in this respect, *fuck* and *shit on* are not dissimilar from imperative verbs and questions. The following are ungrammatical, though synonymous sentences with different surface structures are acceptable:

     (c)
$$\text{Here's that book,} \left\{ \begin{array}{l} \text{which I found interesting.} \\ \text{which I promise to give you.(=a promise)} \\ \text{*which don't read.} \\ \text{which} \left\{ \begin{array}{l} \text{I advise you not to read} \\ \text{I insist that you don't read} \end{array} \right\} \cdot \\ \text{*which I wonder what you think of.} \\ \text{which I would like to know} \left\{ \begin{array}{l} \text{what you think of} \\ \text{your opinion of} \end{array} \right\} \cdot \\ \text{*which what do you think of (it)?} \end{array} \right.$$

Note that the relative clauses in (c) are non-restrictive, in which overt performatives and perhaps declarative sentences have illocutionary force and are grammatical. Commands and questions which have undergone subject deletion and question-word preposing and inversion respectively are not even grammatical. This fact seems closely related to the ungrammaticality of *shit on* and *fuck* in relative clauses. It is an interesting question as to whether restrictive relative clauses are even semantically well-formed, that is, whether the speaker can define something on the basis of his disapproval of it, or whether he can only refer to some definite entity and indicate that he disapproves of it. The only counter-example to the relative clause restriction that I can think of is non-restrictive:

     (d) That's spinach, which the hell with.

Preposing of a question word is impossible in a sentence containing *fuck* or *shit on*. Instead the same order is used as for echo questions, but with different intonation (falling rather than rising).

    (e) Shit on what?
    (f) Fuck the man who invented what?
    (g) *What shit on?
    (h) *What fuck the man who invented?

By the way, I am not going to conclude that the above facts at all contradict Quang's assertions about the syntactic categories of *shit on*, *fuck* etc., but I do think that they indicate that some information is to be found in the murky realm of the performative verb.

[4] British English allows *bloody* as a predicate adjective, but not in those cases where relative clause reduction and adjective preposing could derive Adj N combinations. *Fucking* and *shitting* are never predicate adjectives, in any dialect.

    (a) Don't be bloody.
    (b) He was bloody to me.
    (c) Opening night was bloody. (not synonymous with 'disapproved
    (d) The bloody opening finished us off.   of')

compare (c) and (d) with the synonymous

    (e) Opening night was $\left\{ \begin{array}{l} \text{horrible.} \\ \text{*blasted.} \end{array} \right\}$

    (f) The $\left\{ \begin{array}{l} \text{blasted} \\ \text{*horrible} \\ \text{goddamn} \end{array} \right\}$ opening night finished us off.

[5] Nouns include *shit, fuck*:

    (a) John is a shit.
    (b) That stupid fuck tried to sell me insurance.

I do not see much difference in meaning between (b) and

    (c) That fucking idiot tried to sell me insurance.

Nouns like *shit* and *fuck* referring to persons generally have full stress, and it this regard are unlike unstressed or low-stressed semi-pronominal nouns like *bastard*, which can be used anaphorically. Such use of *fuck* and *shit* sounds odd to me:

    (d) John called and $\left\{ \begin{array}{l} \text{the fúcking idiot} \\ \text{?the stúpid fuck} \\ \text{?the sílly shit} \\ \text{the bastard} \end{array} \right\}$ tried to sell me insurance.

if completely destressed. In view of the fact, noted later, that *fucking* etc. cannot precede an unstressed element, it may be that stressed *fuck* and *shit* in contexts like (d) consist of DISAPPROVED + PRONOUN. If so, then the use of such nouns referring to persons may be an alternative to associating *fucking* with the entire proposition, when the semantic representation associates it with a phonologically unacceptable NP.

[6] Notice here that *fucking* seems to have clear perjorative meaning only in the second clause. This subject will be discussed, or rather evaded, in later sections of the paper.

[7] Compare J. Bltxskrp's insightful remark, 'The mystery and beauty of the English verbal system lies in the fact that the marked member of the opposition has purely privative meaning.'(1938:212).

[8] Normally *fucking* follows numbers, but it precedes names. When a number is an integral part of a name, like the Three Bears, Seven Dwarfs, etc., the whole name includes the number. This also applies to times and sums of money:

    (a)   I waited until $\left\{\begin{array}{l}\text{fucking 4 o'clock in the morning}\\ \text{*4 fucking o'clock in the morning}\end{array}\right\}$

    (b)   You didn't give me $\left\{\begin{array}{l}\text{any fucking ten dollars}\\ \text{?*any ten fucking dollars}\end{array}\right\}$, but I won't

        pay ten fucking dollars for it.

Fucking well versus *fucking* appears with sentences which have *for-to* and *poss-ing* complementizers, with deletion of subjects by Equi-NP-Deletion, showing that S-pruning has not taken place. Plain nominalizations take *fucking*.

[9] Uttered by Mike Kohn in 1961, in you should pardon the word Paris, at a rehearsal of this rather recondite and fey work of W. B. Yeats'. This is probably the genesis of the present work.

[10] See similar copious examples in Jespersen, *Nexus*. pp. 99-101. I am grateful to S. Robbins for bringing this work to my attention.

[11] This conclusion was arrived at somewhat independently of McCawley (1970), where it is presented in very brief form. McCawley is, of course, one of Quang's favorite students.

REFERENCES

Anantalingam, V.S. (1968) 'Up yours' and related constructions. Reprinted in the present volume.

Bltxskrp, Josef. (1938) On the English verbal system. *TCLP* 6:212-489.

Jespersen, O. (1934) *Nexus*. Paris: The Olympia Press.

Lakoff, George. (1968) Pronouns and reference. Unpublished ditto.

Lakoff, George. (1970) *Irregularity in Syntax*. New York: Holt, Rinehart & Winston.

McCawley, James D. (1970) A programme for logic.

Quang Phuc Dong. (1969) Phrases anglaises sans sujet grammatical apparent. *Langages* 14:44-51.

Ross, J.R. (1969) Auxiliaries as main verbs. *Studies in Philosophical Linguistics*, Series One, 77-102.

II. PORNOLINGUISTICS AND SCATOLINGUISTICS

C. Historical and Exotic

K LUČŠE USTANOVLENNOMU GOVNU[1]
(with etymological commentaries)

RENTHGIL

Yelwaccm Semaj, in an article which could be published only in French, was the first to demonstrate two kinds of phucking. Previous to this publication, people had thought there was only one kind of phucking. Now they realized that was only a folk[2] story, and a rash appeared on publications of this type. Hugo Scru, in his "Uvular mechanisms in shared noun phrases (henceforth NP's)", soon showed a third kind of phucking (the so-called "uvula phucking"). Adorukys' unsuccessful attempt to negate these pioneering efforts went so far as to deny the existence of any kind of phucking whatsoever, but was charmingly[3] answered by A. Landers in her sindicated column and in her bucklet "What is French f***ing and is it good or bad for you?" in which she showed that the zero-population-growth-people were really standing behind Adorukys and that in positions like this Greece helps.

And so the rash spread.

Čabnomme, for example, had by now long-since published his famous paper, from which we cite:[4]

> "Drought showed in his grammar of Dnas, a language spoken in the desert, the existence of roughly 69×10^4 different nouns all denoting different kinds of sand. From this fact it was generally concluded that at least 69×10^4 different kinds of sand actually exist in reality. Why, the argument ran, would a language which was up to Drought's work considered natural have 69×10^4 different nouns all denoting different kinds of sand if at least 69×10^4 different kinds of sand didn't actually exist in reality? The famous Czech scholar, Y. K. Smoč, tried to strengthen this argument by showing that "if" could be replaced here by "if and only if". Only Latsop's intervention that his mind boggled followed, and the argument was therefore accepted as valid.[5] Entirely similar are my own results on the Xujstoboju language spoken in New York City at the Institute for Advanced CUNY-Linguists. With the help of a NIVRAG computer I was able to establish in this language the existence of roughly $(3.14159265+) \times 10^{e!}$ different nouns all denoting different kinds of phucking.[6] From this fact I conclude that at least precisely $\pi \times 10^{e!}$ different kinds of phucking actually exist in reality. Why, my argument runs, ..."

Ssor's subsequent publication attempting to show that arguments don't run -- they only walk -- turns out under closer analysis to be simply irrelevant[7] and I have therefore not mentioned it. But an enormous number of highly relevant papers did simply appear, and it began to look as if a large number of different kinds of phucking were at last being established.

With this brief review of the historical antecedents to phucking, I turn now to an interpretation of the phactual data. I show that regardless of how many phucks (or how much phucking) anybody can demonstrate to exist in any natural or unnatural language, there is at a deeper, more abstract level of representation, only one kind of phucking (so-called "abstract phucking"). The demonstration is straightforward:--

Since any given person or any given thing can phuck in only one way at any one given time, all the up-to-now well-established phucks are merely variant forms of the single phuck; allophucks, we might call them. We obviously have here an example of complimentary distribution.[8] It is easy to find cases like the professor the girls the students the university phucks phuck phuck phucks or the last thing she wanted to be dropped was by a flying[9] phuck by him to corroborate this claim.

NOTES

[1] From the IE root $*g^ww-$ and hence related to such English forms as bucolic [Gk bous+kolos], Alexander the Great's celebrated war-horse Bucephalos [Gk bous+kephalē, literally 'ox-head'], butter [Gk bous+tyros; for the semantic relation one thinks also of Skt gávya-, Arm kogi opposite gauh], bovine [Lat bōs, bouis], and so on.

[2] From the IE theme *wl-k-, cf. Lith vilkas ~ Ger Volk from the homophonous theme *wl-k-. Relationship to Lat futuere (whence Fr foutre) uncertain; perhaps from *füken with the vocalism of futuere and the consonantism of Ger ficken?

[3] From the IE root *kn-'sing' and hence related to chant (for n ~ r, see below), hen (literally 'the singer'; cf. Gk ēikanos 'cock', lit. 'singing in the dawn'; Homeric ēōs 'dawn' related to Lat aurōra < *ausōsā by double rhotarirm). Eng charm is from OFr charmer from Lat carmen from *canmen (cf. canō with reduplicated perfect cecinī). Both nm and mn clusters are unstable. Thus from Lat hominem we have *homne > (*homre > Sp hombre. Germanic parallels are not lacking; thus Gothic himins (himn-) reveals dissimilation of the m in Eng heaven, of the n in Ger Himmel. This dissimilation of nasals reminds us of the so-frequent dissimilation of liquids: Eng brabble and blabber but not *brabber or *blabble (cf. Bloomfield, Language, p. 245); Lat nātūrālis, animālis, but not *populālis, *mīlitālis; Russian fevral' 'February' (note that in English, the first r is lacking altogether, a process helped perhaps by January; similar to Feb[r]uaru is lib[r]ary a process hindered perhaps by librárian); Romantic parallels to both dissimilation and truncation are found in Lat arbor, It albero, Sp. árbol, Fr arbre (dial. abre), Lat aratrum, Sp arado; Eng pilgrim (Lat peregrīnus; Gk argaleos, kephalargiā (cf. algos 'pain'); Lat Flōrālia (< *Flōsāsia); and on and on. The nasal dissimilation seems to differ from the liquid dissimilation in that nasals must be juxtaposed, liquids separated by at least one vowel. Perhaps related here is the dissimilation of d's first noted by Varro in Lat meridies < medidies < medius+diēs, although further examples of this particular dissimilation are unknown to me.

[4] This article is reprinted in the present volume, where, however, the word "cement" has been used in place of "sand" for purely structural

reasons.

[5] One does have the impression, however, that the frequency with which
the mind is boggled may well be a not-so-linear function of a rather
different variability-factor. See my forthcoming "A not-so-linear function
of a rather different variability-factor of 3.14159265 [editor's note: the
rest of this footnote was deleted in order to save the space].

[6] Henceforth abbreviated precisely $\pi \times 10^{e}$! For reasons that are now es-
caping from me, this number is sometimes called also the Lewdolphian
number.

[7] The two sharply contrasting views on the source of this word are well
known: (1) Egpt *abu* 'ivory', whence the -ph- in Gk *elephas* 'idem' and
the -b- in Lat *ebur* 'idem' (both presumably from IE *ebh- specified
+foreign) and (2) Gk *hrinokerōs* 'horny-nosed one' [Gk *hrī́s*, *hrī́nos* < *hreō̄*
'flow' + *keras* 'horn'], hence actually related to such forms as *rhinoscopy,
rheum, logorrhoea, catarrh, hemorrhoid* etc. on the one hand, and *corn*
(on the foot, and after *uni-, Capri-* etc.), *horn, hart, cornea, cornucopia,
cerebral* etc., on the other hand. The dispute over the proper etymology
of this word seems to be traceable to the oft-heard (but to my knowledge
mercifully not yet cited in the literature) retort 'It's not irrelevant,
it's a rhinoceros'.

[8] A loan translation from the colloquial French expression 'un exemple
de la distribution complimenteuse'; cf. also 'explanatory adequacy'
from 'la suffisance explicatoise'. I am indebted to my friend and colleague M. Ssorg for these examples.

[9] Etymology of *flying* in this interesting construction is uncertain. On
the other hand, it is clear that *flying* has to do with *birds*, and Ben-
veniste, *Origines*, p. 155, writes that "En partant de gr. αὔρα, on posera
I *ə₂éw-ə₁- : *ə₂w-éə₁- (=*we-) d'où skr. *vā-ti*, etc. L'initiale ₂- de
l'état II *ə₂weə₁- a laissé une trace dans hitt. *ḫuwant* <<vent, tempête>>
(participe de *hwā- = skr. *vā-) ainsi que dans la <<prothèse>> de gr.
ἀϜη-μι. Nous rapportons à cette racine *ə₂ew- le nom de <<l'oiseau>> conçu
soit comme <<aérien>>, soit comme <<rapide>>: neutre *ə₂ewy- > lat.*aui >
auis et adjectif *ə₂w-ei- > skr. *viḥ*, gen. *veḥ*." It may be, then, that
the notion of 'rapidity' is involved in this use of *flying*, an idea supported by the semelfactive [Lat *semel* 'once' < *sm-, cf. Skt *sa-kṛt* 'once']
aspect of the main verb *dropped*.

LEXICAL PROBLEMS RAISED BY
SOME OF THE 'FOUTRE'-CONSTRUCTIONS

MICHEL GOUET
Polytech., Paris, France

In his classical paper on *phuck*, Renthgil correctly derives French *foutre* from the IE theme **wl-k-*. However, this author[1] pretends to demonstrate (against all evidence presented by Q. P. Dong) that the various *phuck*'s have the same underlying form. The argument given is intended to be fairly general, thus one would expect it to apply to French *foutre*. We will indeed show that there are quite a number of *foutres* that cannot be reduced to a single form. More precisely, various syntactic reasons compel French linguists to consider ten different sorts of *foutres*. These *foutres* all have to be considered as independent lexical entries. We present here some basic data on this problem.

The sentence

(1)   Jean fout Marie.

is not ambiguous. Its verb has the following selectional restrictions, given in terms of semantic features:

(i)   subjects must be <+animate, +male>

(*Mon chien fout* $\begin{Bmatrix} Marie \\ Paul \end{Bmatrix}$ are correct sentences, but

*Marie fout Jean)

(ii) direct objects are either <+animate> or <-animate, -male>. The feature "male" is needed independently for contrasting male plugs and female (i.e. <-male>) sockets. A lock is <-male>, while the corresponding key is <+male>.

Sentence (1) can be pronominalized with preverbal pronoun:

(1a) Jean la fout.

and passivized:

(1b) Marie a été foutue par Jean.

We will refer to this *foutre* as *foutre₁*.

Foutre₁ cannot account for the existence of a certain number of other sentence forms whose main verb is also *foutre*. The sentences:

(2) $\begin{cases} \text{Que Marie soit ici} \\ \text{L'attitude de Jean} \\ \text{Cela} \end{cases}$ la fout mal.

have highly restricted subjects.[2] The predicate can be approximately glossed as 'to shock'. The clitic pronoun has no nominal source:

(3) $\begin{Bmatrix} \text{*Que Marie soit ici} \\ \text{*L'attitude de Jean} \\ \text{*Cela} \end{Bmatrix}$ fout mal NP.

and has to be feminine and singular:

(4) $\begin{Bmatrix} \text{*Que Marie soit ici} \\ \text{*L'attitude de Jean} \\ \text{*Cela} \end{Bmatrix} \begin{Bmatrix} \text{les} \\ \text{le} \end{Bmatrix}$ fout mal.

The presence of the adverb *mal* is obligatory:

(5) $\begin{Bmatrix} \text{*Que Marie soit ici} \\ \text{*L'attitude de Jean} \\ \text{*Cela} \end{Bmatrix}$ la fout.

We cannot substitute *bien* for *mal*:

(6) $\begin{Bmatrix} \text{*Que Marie soit ici} \\ \text{*L'attitude de Jean} \\ \text{*Cela} \end{Bmatrix}$ la fout bien.

All these restrictions force us to consider a second verb *foutre*, hence *foutre₂*.

If we now consider the sentence:

(7) Marie est $\begin{Bmatrix} \text{bien} \\ \text{mal} \end{Bmatrix}$ foutue.

we perceive the following ambiguity. The expression (7) has either the meaning of (1b) with adverbial inserts, but without agent, or it can be translated as 'Marie is well/poorly-built'. Subjects in (7) appear to be less restricted than in (1), e.g.:

(8) Cette maison est $\begin{Bmatrix} \text{bien} \\ \text{mal} \end{Bmatrix}$ foutue.

which is not ambiguous; it means only 'This house is well/poorly-built'. In fact, (7) is ambiguous only when its subject belongs to one of the categories of objects defined for (1). We thus have to analyze the new meaning of *foutre* by means of a new *foutre*, called *foutre₃*.

The presence of the adverbials *bien*, *mal* in (7) and (8) raises a new problem. If we consider the sentence

(9) Cette maison est foutue.

it seems to differ from (8) only by the absence of the adverbials. However the relation of the meaning of (9) to the meaning of (8) is unclear. In fact (9) means[3] 'This house is doomed'. We thus introduce a new *foutre*,[4] hence *foutre₄*, stating that *foutre₃* takes an obligatory manner adverbial, as *foutre₂* did. Notice that this phenomenon is not uncommon in French (e.g., *Marie va* vs. *Marie va bien/mal*).

A new sentence type is found with

(10) $\begin{Bmatrix} \text{Marie} \\ \text{Le liquide} \end{Bmatrix}$ fout le camp de cet endroit.[5]

It presents all the symptoms of an idiomatic construction. No noun other than *camp* can be found in the direct object position, and the verbal expression *foutre le camp* is translated as a whole, by the verb *to leave*, for example. The noun phrase *le camp* cannot be pronominalized, and the sentences have no passive. The locative *de cet endroit* is optional and cannot be a noun complement of *camp*. The range of subjects is different from what we have encountered so far in combination with $foutre_p$ ($1 \leq p \leq 4$). We are thus forced to consider that we are dealing here with a $foutre_5$, different from the preceding four.

Consider now

(11) Jean fout $\begin{Bmatrix} \text{la trouille} \\ \text{une gifle} \\ \text{la paix} \end{Bmatrix}$ à Marie.

where *foutre* roughly means 'to give'. This meaning is new.[6] Moreover none of the preceding *foutres* occurs with an indirect object. We must then describe this *foutre* independently of the others, hence $foutre_6$.

In the sentences

(12) Marie se fout de $\begin{Bmatrix} \text{Jean.} \\ \text{ces pompiers.} \\ \text{ce qu'elle soit ici.} \end{Bmatrix}$

the subject is human, and the indirect object is not restricted to any class of *N*'s. It can be a sentential complement. An approximate meaning of (7) is: 'Marie $\begin{Bmatrix} \text{ignores} \\ \text{does not care about} \end{Bmatrix}$ $\begin{Bmatrix} \text{Jean} \\ \text{these firemen} \\ \text{her being here} \end{Bmatrix}$'.

The verb must be constructed reflexively, but there is no possible complement source for the reflexive pronoun:

(13) *NP fout $\begin{Bmatrix} \text{NP} \\ \text{à NP} \end{Bmatrix}$ de NP

where the content of the brackets would correspond to some reflexivizable complement. Moreover the reflexive analysis of *se foutre* derived from *foutre* is both semantically and anatomically unacceptable. (12) is close to forms like

(14) Marie s'étonne de $\begin{Bmatrix} \text{Jean.} \\ \text{ces pompliers.} \\ \text{ce qu'elle soit ici.} \end{Bmatrix}$

but the main difference is that we have for *étonner* the related structure

(15) Qu'elle soit ici étonne Marie.

while

(16) *Qu'elle soit ici fout Marie.

We are thus prevented from deriving this *foutre* from any of the previous ones. We have to consider that this *foutre* is new; we will call it *foutre*[7].

The sentence

(17) Marie est foutue de le faire.
'Marie is capable of doing it.'

has entirely new properties. The infinitive complement may not be replaced by a noun phrase:

(18) *Marie est foutue de NP.

The subject is determined by the infinitive verb, *faire*, which does not seem to be restricted. For example:

(19) Il est foutu de pleuvoir.

(20) Jean est foutu de savoir qu'elle est ici.

This form of *foutre* has thus to be analyzed as an auxiliary (i.e., part of the constituent AUX), or perhaps by raising from a sentential subject. Since it is totally unrelated to the other *foutres*, we name it *foutre*[8].

In the sentence

(21) $\begin{Bmatrix} \text{Jean} \\ \text{Marie} \end{Bmatrix}$ fout ce livre à la poubelle.
'$\begin{Bmatrix} \text{Jean} \\ \text{Marie} \end{Bmatrix}$ throws this book in the garbage can.'

all distributional properties are different from the ones encountered so far. The second complement is obligatory.

(22) $\begin{Bmatrix} \text{*Jean} \\ \text{*Marie} \end{Bmatrix}$ fout ce livre.[7]

We are forced to accept the fact that we are dealing with a new *foutre*, *foutre*[9]. *Foutre*[6] and *foutre*[9] are superficially similar, since they both enter the structure

(23) NP foutre NP à NP.

However, there are important differences in distribution. For example,

(24) *Jean fout la trouille à la poubelle.

Observe that à *NP* is an indirect object with *foutre*[6] but with *foutre*[9] it is a place adverbial that can have other prepositions:

(25) Marie fout ce livre $\begin{Bmatrix} \text{en l'air.} \\ \text{dans sa jupe.} \end{Bmatrix}$

On the other hand, *foutre*[6] and *foutre*[9] present certain similarities. With each of them, according to the nature of the complements, the nature of the subject can vary. We have the following examples of changes:

(26) Jean fout$_6$ $\begin{Bmatrix} \text{la trouille} \\ \text{une gifle} \end{Bmatrix}$ à Marie.

(27) Sa venue fout$_6$ la trouille à Marie.

(28) *Sa venue fout$_6$ une gifle à Marie.

(29) Sa venue fout$_9$ Marie en rage.

(30) *Sa venue fout$_9$ ce livre $\begin{Bmatrix} \text{en l'air.} \\ \text{en rage.} \end{Bmatrix}$

In sentences like

(31) Qu'est-ce que tu $\begin{Bmatrix} \text{fous là?} \\ \text{as foutu de ce livre?} \end{Bmatrix}$

'What the phuck $\begin{Bmatrix} \text{are you doing there?} \\ \text{have you done with that book?} \end{Bmatrix}$,

(32) Je sais ce que tu as foutu.

this use of *foutre* comes very close to the use of the pro-verb *faire* 'do'. It is easy to verify that it cannot be reduced to any of the preceding *foutres* (not even to *foutre$_3$*, which can also be paraphrased by *faire*). Thus we are dealing here with *foutre$_{10}$*.

We have insisted on the differences between all the *foutres*, and these last data emphasize our main point of view. But then how can one consider that in all these varied structures only one *foutre* occurs? We now mention some regularities among the structures, which, in our opinion, make the problem of relating all the *foutres* together even more difficult. First, *foutre$_1$* and *foutre$_9$* both have *mettre* as a synonym: *Jean met Marie* paraphrases (1) and *Marie met ce livre à la poubelle* paraphrases (21). Second, all *foutres* but *foutre$_1$* (i.e., *foutre$_q$*: $2 \leq q \leq 10$), can be replaced by *ficher*. The syntactic properties are all preserved. There is a very slight change in meaning: *ficher* is considered more polite than *foutre*. Notice in this respect that in modern French *foutre$_1$* has a literary flavor,[8] while the *foutre$_q$*'s only occur in slang usage. Finally, *foutre$_2$*, *foutre$_3$*, and *foutre$_9$* have obligatory adverbials. This property is rather infrequent. Should one consider it a coincidence that three unrelated verbs, with a common morphemic shape, have a syntactic property in common as well?

The situation we just described is fairly general. Given a verb, it very often has various uses that cannot be related by transformations, although its various forms share some common meaning. Generative semantics cannot cope with this situation. Postal, in his description of *remind*, failed to describe the use of *remind* in *John reminded Paul that he had to leave*. In the present case, we also do not see how generative semantics could derive the noun *foutre* 'sperm' from *foutre$_1$*. Obviously, the verb *foutre* and the noun *foutre* are related, but the problem of including the mening of the noun *foutre* in the description of the verb *foutre* cannot be solved within the framework of generative semantics, nor within any existing framework.

The types of examples presented here should urge linguists to discover new theories (and new *foutres*) if they want to account for all the regularities.

NOTES

[1] I am deeply indebted to Renthgil M. T. for many helpful suggestions that considerably strengthened the argument that I present here.

[2] One also finds human nouns in subject positions:

(i)   Jean la fout mal.

Such sentences are ambiguous with either the interpretation of (1a) where the subject is "active" or with the approximate paraphrase

(ii)   L'attitude de Jean la fout mal.

and *Jean* would not be "active".

[3] If we read more carefully (7) and (8), we can perceive that they also have this additional meaning, presumably blurred by the semantic incompatibility of the adverbials with *foutue* (cf., the strangeness of *well doomed, poorly doomed*). This observation strengthens our analysis of (9).

[4] *Foutre$_3$* and *foutre$_4$* are only found in passive-like forms.

[5] The imperative forms have the peculiarity of accepting the so-called expletive pronoun *moi* as in

(i) $\begin{Bmatrix} \text{Fous} \\ \text{Foutez} \end{Bmatrix}$ - $\begin{Bmatrix} \text{moi} \\ \text{nous} \end{Bmatrix}$ le camp.

But notice

(ii) *Fous-$\begin{Bmatrix} \text{toi} \\ \text{lui} \\ \text{vous} \\ \text{leur} \end{Bmatrix}$ le camp.

(iii) *Marie $\begin{Bmatrix} \text{me} \\ \text{te} \\ \text{...} \end{Bmatrix}$ fout le camp.

(iv) *Marie fout le camp à $\begin{Bmatrix} \text{moi.} \\ \text{Jean.} \end{Bmatrix}$

In this respect, we also observe the form *Foutre Dieu!* 'Good phucking Lord!'(?), which is not an imperative since *foutre* is in infinitive form. Nor can it be the noun *foutre*, for it could not have *Dieu* as an apposition. Presumably *foutre* is here the infinitive *foutre$_1$*, but it is not clear whether *Dieu* is its subject or its object.

[6] We consider the highly lexicalized sentence type:

(i)   Il en fout plein la vue à Marie.

contains *foutre$_6$*, although its meaning may be distant from the meaning of (11) (i.e., *He shows off in front of Mary*). We analyze it with *en* as having its source in some specific direct object, and *plein la vue* is a locative. We take the same position for

(ii) Je t'en foutrai, moi, des bijoux!

as a very negative answer from *je* (emphasized by *moi*) to a request for jewels (*en*, emphasized by *des bijoux*), made by *t'*. Here *foutre* is clearly synonymous with *donner*.

[7] In fact, *Jean fout ce livre* can be interpreted with *foutre$_1$* (cf. Scarry (1967) for such a deviant example).

[8] *Foutre$_1$* can be used virtually only in poetry; a typical example is the following, from Baudelaire (1954):

...- de plus, il peut foutre
Debout comme un singe avisé.
. ...

REFERENCES

Baudelaire, C. (1954) La civilisation belge (Amenitates Belgicae). In *Oeuvres complètes*. Paris: La Pléiade.

Postal, Paul. (1970) On the surface verb 'remind'. *Linguistic Inquiry* 1:37-120.

Quang, P. D. (1969) Phrases anglaises sans sujet grammaticale apparent. *Langages* 14:44-51.

Renthgil, (1971) K lušče ustanovlennomu govnu (with etymological commentaries). In the present volume.

Scarry, R. (1967) *Egg in the Hole Book*. New York: Golden Press.

AN EXAMPLE OF ICONICITY IN RUSSIAN

BILL J. DARDEN
University of California, Berkeley

The Russian verb *bzdet'*, daintily defined in Dal' (1903) as: *tixo, bez šuma ispuskat' vetry iz života, prtvpl. perdet', delat' to že samoe gromko* (quietly, without sound, emit winds from the stomach; opposed to *perdet'*, do the same thing loudly), is morphophonemically unique. It is the only verb in Russian to preserve the voiced palatal stop which comes from a /dj/ cluster; i.e., it has first sing. pres. *bzdžu*, presumably pronounced /bžǯu/.[1] Other verbs in -*zd*- lose the stop, although they may optionally retain the "soft" (less strident) pronunciation of the geminate *žž*, e.g. *ezdit'*, *ežžu* /ježǯu/ /ježžu/. Preceded by anything other than /z/, /d/ becomes strident /ž/, e.g. *perdet'*, *peržu*. The simplified (and slightly incorrect) morphophonemics is:

		bzd-e-i-u	ezd-i-i-u	perd-e-i-u
1.	Vowel truncation	bzd-i-u	ezd-i-u	perd-i-u
2.	i → j / __ V	bzd-j-u	ezd-j-u	perd-j-u
3.	dj → ǯ	bzǯu	ezǯu	perǯu
4.	z → ž / __ ǯ	bžǯu	ežǯu	--
5.	ǯ → ž	--	ežžu	peržu
6.	ž → ž	--	ežžu	peržu

(optional is geminate, never before a palatal stop)

The ǯ → ž rule does not apply to *bzdžu*, and it is our task to discover why. A naive phonologist might suggest that since *bzdet'* is the only instance of a /zd/ cluster preceded by another consonant, that this is the conditioning factor. Anyone who believes that can skip the rest of this paper.[2] We might also try to attribute the difference in the phonology to the relatively low stylistic level to which *bzdet'* belongs. However, the alternation is regular in *perdet'*, and, in any reasonable society, loud farts must be considered lower style than silent farts. A purist might suggest that we throw out *bzdet'*, since it is only in Dal' not in any of the standard dictionaries of the literary language. But this is also true of *perdet'*, as well as *srat'* 'shit' and *eti* 'fuck'. Anyone who doubts their literary status should read Puškin and Solzenicyn. The only real justification for throwing out *bzdet'* would be empirical evidence that Russians have ceased to fart silently.

The purpose of this paper is to show that the failure of the ǯ → ž rule to operate in *bzdet'* is and results in an iconic representation of the semantic opposition between *bzdet'* and *perdet'*. By iconicity we mean factual similarity between signans and signatum. The term is taken from Shapiro (1969), who took it from Jakobson (1965), who took it from Pierce (1931:134-173). To quote Shapiro (1969:7-8): "Jakobson emphasizes, after Pierce, the division of icons into three distinct subclasses: images, diagrams, and metaphors. Images are characterized by a relation between signans and signatum in which the former contains the simple qualities of the latter. Diagrams are characterized by a relation between signans and signatum which is constituted solely by the relations

87

of their parts. Finally, metaphors embody the representative character of the signans by exhibiting a parallelism in the signatum."

Onomatopoeia is a common type of iconic imagery in language. Both *bzdet'* and *perdet'* are onomatopoeic. *Bzdet'* means 'to go bzzzz'; *perdet'* means 'to go prrrr'(Russia r's, not English ones). Both words have Indo-European sources;[3] *perdet'* is cognate with *fart*. The similarity between the two words is more marked in Proto-Slavic, where they differ by only one segment: **pьzděti pьrděti*. It is clear that the basic opposition was and is 'hissing fart' vs. 'rumbling fart'. It is appropriate and iconic that both begin with a bilabial release. It would perhaps be more appropriate if *perdet'* contained a bilabial trill rather than an *r*, but language has to do the best it can within the constraints of its phonology.

The modern Russian forms have further developed iconic parallels to the semantic opposition. For instance, the assyllabicity of the root in *bzdet'* vs. the full sonorance of *perd-* parallels the distinction in volume of sound. More important for this paper is the opposition which results from the failure of the $\acute{z} \rightarrow \acute{z}$ rule to operate on *bzdžu*. We can easily discern iconic parallels between the $\acute{z}/\acute{z}$ opposition and the silent/loud opposition in farts. In Russian the palatal stop $\check{c}$, /ć/, is less strident than the palatal continuants /š/ and /ž/. Although Dal' gives no phonetics (see note 1), we may assume that this single instance of a voiced palatal stop is also non-strident /$\acute{ǰ}$/. The optional non-strident pronunciation /jeǯžu/ provides evidence for this,[4] as does the word *doždʹ* 'rain' (underlying doźź) which with final devoicing may be pronounced /dość/. The strident/mellow oppositon is defined acoustically (Jakobson and Halle, 1956:31) as "higher intensity noise vs. lower intensity noise." Since the strident consonant shows up in the word for the noisier fart, we have a clear case of iconic imagery.

Finally, the very blocking of the rule can be interpreted as an iconic metaphor. David Stampe has insightfully characterized the blocking of a rule as the acquisition of a phonological inhibition. In order to articulate *bzdžu*, then, a Russian must inhibit a natural process. Of the two actions signified by the words, it is obvious that loud farting is the less inhibited.

Thus, having demonstrated the parallels between the opposition of the less noisy, inhibited /$\acute{ǰ}$/ to the noisier, less inhibited /ž/ and the opposition of the quieter, inhibited *bzdenie* to the loud, uninhibited *perdenie*, we have an accounting of the seeming irregularity in *bzdžu* which has true explanatory value. We can only hope that the success of this venture will encourage others to investigate the effect of semantics on the phonological component of a grammar.

NOTES

[1] Dal' does not describe the phonetics, and all the Russian informants consulted claimed that the verb was not attested in the first singular in their speech.

[2] I would welcome comment on the possibility of this being true. Perhaps

the retention of the stop actually breaks up the cluster, with resultant semi-syllabicity of ž.

[3] The folk etymology which links *bzdet'* to *pizda* 'vagina' is lamentably incorrect.

[4] Avanesov (1968:151) states that in the speech of individuals, one occasionally finds standard /žž/ pronounced /žǯ/, although this pronunciation cannot be considered 'orthoepic.' Jakobson (1948:161 fn.11) must be one of those individuals, since he describes /zd/ and /zg/ as alternating with žǯ (his phonemic representation of /žǯ/).

REFERENCES

Avanesov, R. I. (1968) *Russkoe literaturnoe proiznošenie*. Moscow: Procveščenie.

Dal', V. (1903) *Tolkovyj slovar' živogo velikorusskago jazyka*. St. Petersburg: Vol'f.

Jakobson, R. (1948) Russian conjugation. *Word* 4:155-67.

Jakobson, R. and M. Halle. (1956) *Fundamentals of Language*. The Hague: Mouton & Co.

Jakobson, R. (1965) Quest for the essence of language. *Diogenes* 51:21-37.

Pierce, C. S. (1931) *Collected Papers*. vol. 2. ed. C. Hartshorne and P. Weiss. Cambridge, Mass.: Harvard University Press.

Shapiro, M. (1969) *Aspects of Russian Morphology*. Cambridge, Mass.: Slavica.

Vasmer, M. (1953) *Russisches etymologisches Wörterbuch*. Heidelberg: Carl Winter.

UN BOUQUET FRANÇAIS

ANN DAINGERFIELD ZWICKY
University of Illinois

Mr. Darden has shown an excellent insight into the imitative nature of words for farting. The iconic imagery involved in words for farting is even more accurate than conventional definitions would lead us to believe, for both words denoting "noisy" farting and those for "noiseless" farting are accurately onomatopoetic. That is, both imitate sounds. This characterization contradicts the usual distinction drawn between kinds of farts, but I believe a careful examination of the evidence drawn from French will, in conjunction with the Russian evidence presented by Mr. Darden, be sufficient to show convincingly that the real distinction represented is not between noisiness and noiselessness, but between different kinds of noise. Farts are not linguistically represented as sounding or silent, but as explosive or hissing.[1] The historically inaccurate definitions current in dictionaries have come about because of the relatively greater loudness of the explosive fart.

French, like Russian, possesses two series of words for farts and farting; pet, péter and their derivatives, versus vesse and vesser. The masculine noun pet(<Lat. pēditum < pēdere) is defined by the Petit Larousse as: "Gaz qui sort du fondement avec bruit." The feminine noun vesse, on the other hand, is defined as: "Emission de gaz fétides, faite sans bruit par l'anus." It is notable that vesse and vesser are marked in the Larousse as "populaire", while pet and péter carry no such stigma, and are indeed perfectly respectable French words. According to Bloch and von Wartburg (1968), the creampuff or pet-de-nonne was euphemized into respectability at the end of the 18th century from its raffish identity as the pet-de-putain before that date; nobody has yet found it necessary to change the first element to a hiccough or a sigh. One can only conjecture that the vesse lost its respectability as a hissing fart by lapsing into official silence, as this change introduces the element of fetidity -- "gaz fétides" -- as part of its identification. One may speak with propriety of a noise, even a rude noise, but not of a foul smell, particularly if it emanates involuntarily from oneself or one's companions. In a more puritanical society the fart which becomes silent may lose its identity entirely. The English fyste, with which Cotgrave's 16th Century French-English dictionary (1611) glossed vesse, survives now only in feist and feisty, words which apply only to dogs and have no reference to gaseous emissions.

The verb péter, according to the Petit Larousse, means not only "faire un pet", but also "faire un bruit subit et éclatant" -- a motorcycle, for example, pète. The series of pet-derivatives carries on the theme of explosiveness. A pétarade is a "Suite de pets que fait un cheval en ruant" or a "suite de détonations". Similarly, the name of the cane-petière, a sort of white-collared duck, is explained by Bloch and von Wartburg as deriving from cane + pétière, by suffixal alternation from péteuse,[2] because "quand il fuit, il se déleste et produit ainsi des petits bruits."[3] Even more significantly, a pétard is defined by the P. Larousse as "Petite pièce d'artifice que l'on fait exploser soit pour produire un effet de démolition ou de rupture, soit pour provoquer un bruit (signaux, réjouissances)." *Pétiller*, which shows the diminutive and repetitive verbal suffix *-iller* (cf. *mordiller* < *mordre*) means primarily: "Eclater en produisant de petit: bruits qui se succèdent rapidement: *bois, charbon, qui pétille.*"[3]

Buck's (1965) *Selected Synonyms* lists both *péter*, the explosive fart of the French, and *bzdet'*, the hissing fart of the Russians, as derivatives of the same IE root, **pezd* or **bzd*, which is said to be "of imitative origin, but probably through 'blow'." The meaning difference between *péter* and *bzdet'* must then be directly attributable to the different phonological evolution of the two languages. *Péter*, in contrast to *bzdet'*, contains no voiced consonants and no spirants. Pierre Delattre (1966:111-119) establishes a hierarchy of articulatory force for French consonants, in which *p, t, k* rank highest of all simple consonants. This means, by Delattre's definition, that *e* followed by *t* is maximally shortened. *P* and *t* are both classed by Delattre as explosives; the voiceless bilabial is probably the most explosive of the French consonants. It would be better if it were aspirated, but, as Darden points out, "language has to do the best it can within the constraints of its phonology."

Vesse and *vesser*, like *pet* and *péter*, are classed by Buck as being "probably of imitative origin." As in the case of the **pezd* derivatives, he suggests a relationship to "blow", and in this case perhaps to Lat. *spirāre* 'breathe' and OCS *peskati* 'whistle'. *Vesse* and *vesser*, unlike *péter*, belong to a group of words all of which show two fricatives. Buck does not suggest a common root for these words, but there is very little divergence in their consonantal elements. *V* is classified by Delattre in the class of weakest articulation -- weaker than *f*, by virtue of its voicing -- and corresponds as closely as any fricative to the bilabial articulation of *p*. The *s* is "sifflant" -- the perfect hiss.

Due presumably to their lack of respectability, *vesse* and *vesser* show no derived forms in normal dictionaries and participate in only one compound -- the *vesse-de-loup* or puffball mushroom.[4] It is interesting to note that the *pet-de-loup*, which also exists, is a "type de vieux professeur ridicule."

NOTES

[1] I have chosen the opposition of explosive vs. hissing rather than Darden's rumbling/hissing distinction because it more closely fits the phonological and etymological facts in French.

[2] "Due sans doute à un euphémisme" -- although I can't imagine why ducks call for more delicacy in this regard than other creatures.

[3] Its secondary meaning: "Mousser, dégager des bulles de gaz," bears an amusing but probably accidental further resemblance to the present verb; the tiny explosions are more important than their gaseous cause.

[4] According to Cotgrave the 16th Century English could call this comestible

fungus a "wolve's fyste," or several other even less savory-sounding things since vanished from the language.

REFERENCES

Bloch, O. and W. von Wartburg. (1968) *Dictionnaire etymologique de la langue française.* Paris: Presses Universitaires de France.

Buck, C. D. (1965) *A Dictionary of Selected Synonyms in the Principal Indo-European Languages.* Chicago: University of Chicago Press.

Cotgrave, Randle. (1611) *A Dictionarie of the French and English Tongues.* (Reproduced from the first edition). Columbia, S.C.: University of South Carolina Press.

Delattre, Pierre. (1951) *Principes de phonétique française.* Middlebury: Middlebury College.

Delattre, Pierre. (1966) *Studies in French and Comparative Phonetics.* The Hague: Mouton & Co.

THE PREFIXED FORMS OF LATVIAN PIST 'FUTUERE'

ANDRZEY LURBA
University of Pinsk

Latvian lexicography has been strangely remiss in providing documentation for the verb *pist* (stem *pis-*). Only a few items of the derivational complex have made their way into the *Latviešu valodas vārdnīca** (namely, *izpist, izpisties, nuopisties, papist, papisties, uzpist, uzpisējs, piselīgs, pisēties, pisināt, pisīgs, pislis, pist, pisties, pisējs, pisiens,* and *pisarainis*). The gap is not easily remedied. Latvian *belles lettres* do not seem to employ the word; folklore texts are strangely unimaginative (the basic verb occurs, to be sure, but the prefixed verbs do not); and basic informant work has not been done (nor can be started in the present fiscal crisis). The purpose of this article is to provide some hints for a basic outline that may serve as a start toward the beginnings of a first step toward a point where we may hope to see the first glimmerings of some small understanding of the semantic complexities involved. The material is presented in the form of lexical entries. The verb *pist* is presented first, followed by *nuopist* and *izpist*, since the perfectivizing *nuo-* and *iz-*, for this verb, seem to be most nearly semantically empty, primarily providing a perfective counterpart to the imperfective base verb. The intransitive *pisties* is listed next, along with its perfectives *izpisties* and *nuopisties*. The remaining prefixed forms, all perfective, are given in an alphabetical order.

pist v.t., imperf., 'to fuck' (i.e. someone).

nuopist v.t., perf., 'to fuck' (involving the passive partner's satisfaction).

izpist v.t., perf., 'to fuck' (involving the passive partner's dissatisfaction). In some locutions this verb approximates the meanings of English *to be screwed* or *to be had*.

pisties v.i., imperf., 1. 'to fuck'; 2. vulg. 'to be ineffectively occupied!.

nuopisties v.i., perf., 1. 'to have a (hearty) fuck'; 2. 'to fuck fuck oneself into the blind staggers of physical and monetary exhaustion'; 3. vulg. 'to waste a stretch of time in being ineffectively occupied'.

izpisties v.i., perf., 'to fuck to one's heart's content'. Note that the intransitive verb does not have the hostile overtones of *izpist*.

appist v.t., perf., 1. 'to spray with semen'; 2. 'to swindle'.

appisties v.i., perf., 'to get traces of sexual discharge all over oneself'.

aizpist v.t., perf., 'to partially fuck s.-o.; to pre-fuck'.

aizpisties v.i., perf., 1. 'to lose track [of time, etc.] while
  fucking'; 2. vulg. 'to wander off to someone's inconvenience
  without telling where to'.

atpist v.t., perf., 'to alienate by fucking'.

atpisties v.t., perf., 1. 'to fuck to the point where one loses
  taste for it'; 2. vulg. 'to get lost' (primarily in the
  imperative *atpisies!* 'fuck off!').

iepist v.t., perf., 1. 'to fuck into' (e.g., a bottle); 2. 'to
  break in by fucking'

iepisties v.i., perf., 1. 'to get warmed up or skilled by fucking';
  2. 'to fuck one's way into'; 3. vulg. 'to show up in some
  enclosure (e.g., the farm-yard) unexpectedly and without
  welcome'.

papist v.t., perf., 1. 'to fuck for a while' (with overtones of
  inattention or lack of resolve); 2. vulg. 'to lose'.

papisties v.i., perf., 'to fuck (around) for a while'.

pārpist v.t., perf., 'to overfuck'.

pārpisties v.i., perf., 'to overfuck'.

piepist v.t., perf., 1. 'to fuck full'; 2. vulg. 'to cheat or
  swindle'.

piepisties v.i., perf., vulg. 'to become an unexpected unwelcome
  companion'.

sapist v.t., perf., vulg. 'to ruin beyond repair'.

sapisties v.i., perf., vulg. 'to enter into a sexual or social
  misalliance'.

uzpist v.t., perf., 'to fuck' (with competence and, possibly,
  on demand).

uzpisties v.i., perf., vulg. 'to become an unexpected and persistent pest'.

In examining the above list, a number of very surprising observations are immediately apparent. For one, there do not seem to be any
calques from Greek or Latin, of the *atlikt* 'postpone' (lit. 'off-put')
variety. There is also a striking reluctance for most of the above verbs
to be negated; thus, while *nepārpisties* 'to not overfuck' is a perfectly
good form, comparable forms, e.g., *neatpisies!* 'do not fuck off! (i.e.,
'do not get lost')' are barely, if at all, possible. There is a striking
absence of local meanings (with the exception of the somewhat unlikely

iepist); although the prefixes can have local meanings, such meanings simply do not occur; thus *aizpist* does not occur with the potential meanings 'to fuck away' or 'to fuck up to'. Finally, let us note that some of the meanings are parasitic, in the sense that a more neutral verb has been replaced by the strongly emotive *pist*. Thus, *aizpisties* in its second meaning replaces the more neutral *aizkulties* or *aizdauzī-ties*, and, to a degree, the meaning of *aizpisties* depends on the existence of the more neutral verbs. An English parallel would be the (imaginary) replacement of *He's gotten lost* by *He's gotten, the fuck, lost* and in turn by *He's fucked off*.

NOTE

* K. Müllenbachs and J. Endzelīns, *Latviešu valodas vārdnīca* (4 vols.; Rīga, 1923-1932); J. Endzelīns and E. Hauzenberga, *Papildinājumi un labojumi K. Mülenbacha Latviešu valodas vārdnīcai* (2 vols.; Rīga, 1934-1946).

ON THE RUSSIAN VERB "EBÁT'" AND SOME OF ITS DERIVATIVES

RICHARD C. DeARMOND
Simon Fraser University

1. Some phonological notes

The verb *ebát'*, which literally means 'to fuck', and figuratively
'to curse, to discipline', is composed of the root /eb/ plus either no
thematic suffix or the thematic suffix *a*.[1] The underlying
form of the suffix which we posit here, and some of the rules which we
employ here are based on the arguments in DeArmond (forthcoming). The
arguments relevant to this paper are briefly summarized below.

Verb stems which terminate in *a* or *aj*[2] have not been considered to
be related, but simply treated as different classes of stems. We note,
however, that there are several pairs of verbs which alternate between *a*
and *aj*; for example, *rýska, rýskaj* 'race about, roam'. These two stems
differ in the present tense and the imperative, but not in the past or the
infinitive; for example, the first person singular is respectively: *rýšču,
rýskaju*; similarly: *kápa, kápaju* 'drip, pour slowly' (the latter is colloquial): *káplju, káplaju*. We further note that the majority of verb stems
which terminate with the thematic suffix *aj* have stress fixed on the suffix,
or except for a predictable subclass of stems, the stress occurs on the
root of only a few stems. Stems with *ā* fall into two classes: root stress
and mobile stress. Because of phonological similarity, and because of the
tendency for one class to be replaced with the other but less frequently
for it to be replaced with the remaining classes, we find it preferable to
classify both together; we assign fixed stress to those stems where stress
remains fixed. Thus to verbs such as *igráj* 'play', *letáj* 'fly', and *ebáj*
'fuck', we assign fixed stress; to such verbs as *pláka* 'cry' we assign root
stress, and we consider verbs such as *pisa* 'write' to be unmarked for stress.
A phonological rule will place the stress on the ending in the first person
singular, on the root in the remaining non-past tense forms, and on the
thematic suffix in the past tense. We also note further that [j][3] occurs
before underlying front vowels in verbs with *aj*. In verbs with *a* [j] alter-
nates with [a]; [j] occurs before underlying front vowels, and [a] before
consonants (the past tense and the infinitive). Thus we posit the underlying shape of both *a* and *aj* to be /ō/, where [j] is predictable, and we
posit a rule which laxes /ō/, if it is not stressed, and then deletes it
under certain conditions:
all monophonematic suffixes (/ā, ē, ī/) become lax if they are not stressed.
If both [o] and [e] occur unstressed in consecutive suffixes, we state by
a rule that [o] is deleted. Thus the underlying forms of the verbs previously mentioned are /igr+ō´/ 'play', /let+ō´/ 'fly', /eb+ō´/ 'fuck',
/plō´k+ō/ 'cry', and /pīs+ō/ 'write'. In /rū´sk+ō/ 'race about' and
/kō´p+ō/ 'drip' an optional minor rule prevents the suffix from becoming
lax. In /dóum+ō/ the aforementioned minor rule is mandatory.

Other verbal thematic suffixes may also be similarly classed.

e and *ej* both occur in intransitive verbs with few exceptions; *ej* most frequently occurs with inchoative deadjectival verbs and sometimes with denominal verbs; *e* is frequently the imperfective counterpart of momentary onomonopoeic verbs in *nu*: *skripé* 'squeak, creak' (imperfective), *skrípnu* (perfective momentary). The stress occurs on the thematic suffix of the vast majority of verbs which terminate in *ej* and *e*. In some verbs the stress occurs on the root with *ē*:*víde* 'see' (which is also transitive), and rarely with *ej*: *berémenej* 'become pregnant'. Also rare are verbs with *e* which have mobile stress: *smotre* 'look at'; *smotrjú* and *smótriš'* (first and second person singular). We may thus posit /ē/ as the underlying thematic suffix for both sub-classes, where /ḗ/ remains tense if stressed. /blad+in+ḗ/ 'become pale': *bladnéju* 'I am becoming pale'. /boud+ḗ/ 'keep awake', and /moul+ḗ/ 'be thrilled with'. If the thematic suffix is unstressed, it becomes lax: /skrip+ē/: *skrípit* 'it is squeaking', /ui´de+ē/: *vídit* 'he sees'.

    Verbs with the suffix *i* fall into three stress classes: root-fixed /kréuk+ī/, suffix fixed /gouor+ī́/ 'speak', and mobile: /leubi+ī/ 'love' -- *ljubljú* and *ljúbiš'* "first and third person singular, respectively). Thus /ī/ can be grouped with /ō/ and /ē/; the remaining suffixes, both simple (*nu*) and compound (/ou+ā/) show two types: stem stress and suffix stress; in the suffix *yv+aj* the stress occurs on the syllable immediately preceding the suffix: /roz+robō´t+u+ɔ/ 'cultivate, exploit'. Verb stems in /ī/ differ from those in /ō/ and /ē/" epenthetic [j] does not occur before front vowels: /gouor+ī´+e+m/ → [gəvar,ü´] 'I speak', not [gəvar,íjü].

    The verb stress in unmarked 'ī' stems is mobile, presumably to maintain a distinction between it and the suffix-stress types (which have otherwise identical suffixes), whereas in 'ē' verbs which are unmarked stress remains fixed. However, in unmarked stems in 'ō' the stress is mobile except for a few predictable subtypes: /dō+ō/ 'give' (imperfective), *dajú* and *daéš'* (first and second persons singular). It is not clear why this class should have mobile stress.

    In certain stems with /ē/ the thematic suffix remains lax but the stress occurs on the root. The stress in these stems is generally predictable; for example, in all verbs with the suffixes /in+īk+ē/ the stress occurs on the syllable preceding the suffixes or elsewhere on the root if the stress occurs on that syllable in its derivant: *sabotážničat'* 'practice sabotage'. *portnjáničat'* 'be a tailor', which is derived from *portnój* 'tailor', and *vétreničat'* 'behave frivolously', which is derived from *vétrenik* 'frivolous person'.

    Ebat' is the only known verb where the thematic suffix alternates with no suffix as a lexical variant. If the verb stem is without a thematic suffix, it is unmarked for stress. The vast majority of such verbs are so marked. The non-past tense suffix /e/ is attached to the stem, and to it the personal desinences; or the past tense suffix /l/ is attached to the stem, and to /l/ are attached desinences marking gender and number, which are in agreement with the subject of the verb. The infinitive of the non-thematic stem[4] is *et'*; the occurrence of the stress on the root instead of the suffix is irregular; the expected place of stress is on the ending: *etí*.

A few examples of the conjugation of *et'/ebát'* are given below, including a brief description of the relevant rules. Stress is assigned to the unmarked stem on the suffix marking tense if vocalic, or it occurs on the only vowel in the suffix. Thus the first person singular /eb+e+m/ → [eb+é+m]. Epenthetic [j] is inserted immediately before word initial /e/; [jeb+é+m]. /e/ becomes rounded and back [o] by a rule which labializes /e/ before a nasal plus a word boundary [jeb+ó+m] (or before a nasal plus another consonant as in the third person plural [jeb+ó+ntu], but not in the first person plural [jeb+é+mu]). [o] becomes nasalized when it occurs in a syllable closed with a nasal: [jeb+õ´+m], and the word final nasal is deleted: [jeb+õ´]. Denasalization and subsequent raising of the back vowel follow: [jeb+ú], and /e/ is replaced with [i] if unstressed (*ikan'je*): [jibú] 'I am fucking'.

In addition to the above rules which are applicable to the third person singular (/eb+e+tu/ → [eb+é+tu] → [jeb+é+tu]), consonants before front vowels are palatalized [jeb,+é+tu], final lax high vowels are deleted [jeb,+é+t], and /e/ becomes rounded but remains non-back before unpalatalized consonants, which are velarized and labialized: [jeb,+ö+t]→ [jib,+ö+t] (*ikan'je*) 'he fucks'.

In the past tense masculine singular /eb+l+u/, stress is assigned to the vocalic desinence: [eb+l+ú], epenthetic [j] occurs: [jeb+l+ú], final lax high vowels are deleted with concomitant retraction of stress: [jéb+l], final [l] is deleted following a consonant plus a morpheme boundary: [jeb], [e] becomes rounded [jöb], and final consonants become voiceless: [jöp] 'I have fucked'.

In the past tense feminine singular /eb+l+õ/, stress is assigned to the vocalic desinence and does not retract: [eb+l+õ´/; epenthetic [j] occurs: [jeb+l+õ´], [õ] is replaced with [a]: [jeb+l+á], and *ikan'je* follows: [jib+l+á] 'she fucks' (if such a form is possible in Russian; see below).

In the imperative /eb+oi/ the suffix is stressed and epenthetic [j] occurs: [jeb+ói]. By a rule reversal [oi] becomes fronted before [ei] is raised to [ii] → [í] (otherwise [oi] → [ei] → [ē] after [ei] → [ii]): [jeb+éi] → [jeb+íi] → [jeb+í´]. Consonants are palatalized before front vowels: [jeb,+í´]. In the infinitive /eb+tei/ the stress occurs irregularly on the root: [éb+tei] → [jéb+tei] (epenthetic [j]), under certain conditions, unstressed [e] in the suffix is deleted (this rule may be a part of the law of the open syllable): [jé+ti] → [jet,+i] (palatalization of consonants before front vowels). Final lax high vowels are deleted: [jét,] 'to fuck'.

If the stem occurs with the suffix /õ´/, epenthetic [j] is inserted between a stressed vowel and another vowel, providing the former is not /í/. [eb+o´+e+m] → [jeb+õ´+e+m]. After labialization [o] becomes fronted following a palatal consonant: [jeb+õ´j+o+m] → [jeb+õ´j+ö+m] → [jeb+õ´j+ȫm]→ [jeb+õ´j+õ] → [jib+õ´+ü] → [jeb+áj+ü] → [jib+áj+ü] 'I am fucking'.

The third person singular non-past requires no extra rules: /eb+õ⁴+e+tu/ → /jeb+õ⁴+e+tu/ → [jeb+õ´j+e+tu] → [jeb+áj+e+tu] → [jeb+áj+e+t] → [jib+áj+i+t] 'he is fucking'. No extra rules are necessary for the past tense: /eb+ō´+l+u/ → [jeb+ō´+l+u] → [jeb+ō´+l] → [jeb+á+l] → [jib+á+l]. The infinitive also requires no extra rules: /eb+ō´+tei/ → [jeb+ō´+tei] → [jeb+ō´+t,ei] → [jeb+á+t,ei] → [jeb+á+t,i] → [jeb+á+t,] → [jib+a+t,]. In the imperative /eb+ō´+oi/ [oi] becomes fronted before the jod epenthesis rule: [eb+ō´+ei] → [jeb+ō´j+ei] → [jeb+ō´j+i] (unstressed [e] is deleted under certain conditions) → [jeb+áj+i] → [jeb+áj] → [jib+áj].

Note that in /pīs+ō/ 'write',which is unmarked for stress, tense /ō/ becomes lax (it is unstressed): /pīs+ō+e+m/ → [pis+ōj+e+m] → [p‚ɪs+ōj+e +m] → [p,is+oj+e+m]. If the stem is unmarked, the first person becomes stressed. The stressing rule occurs after the subrule which deletes [o], if both [o] and [e] occur unstressed in the desinences: [p,ɪs+j+e+m] → [p,ɪs+j+é+m] → [p,ɪs+j+ó+m] → [p,ɪs+j+ö´+m] → [p,ɪs+j+ö´m] → [p,ɪs+j+ö´] → [p,ɪs+j+ü´] → [p,iš+ü´] → [p,iš,+u´] → [p,iš+ú] ([š,], [ž,], and [c,] become non-palatalized) 'I am writing'. [sj] is replaced with [š] (jod palatalization).

2. Some syntactic and semantic notes about *ebát'*

Quang (1966) states that *fuck* in English is a true verb in one sense (to copulate), and a quasi-verb in the other as in *fuck you!* Because of the misinterpreted translation of the Russian expression

(1) Ëb tvojú mat'.

it has usually been assumed that the verb *ebát'* is a quasi-verb also, since it is frequently translated as

(1a) Fuck your mother.

However, this is not the correct or literal translation. The form *ëb* is not an imperative; it is the masculine singular past tense form of the verb /eb/, the derivation of which was discussed above. Sentence (1) literally means

(1b) I have fucked your mother.

The imperfective aspect here may imply that the event has occurred more than once, which, we presume, is more derogatory than if the perfective form of the verb were used. On the other hand *ebát'* frequently serves as a strong expletive expressing anger, surprise, or condemnation. When used frequently as a parenthetical expression by foul-mouthed speakers it has no specific meaning, but serves as a linguistic condiment expressing contempt. It is for this reason that (1) may be figuratively translated as (1b) in English, since it expresses roughly the same degree of contempt to an English speaker as (1) does to a Russian speaker. Despite the figurative translation of (1) into English, the verb *ebát'* nevertheless remains a true verb in Russian. Some other expressions exist in Russian which do not have any known equivalent figurative translations in English but they are nevertheless offensive when translated:

(2) Žit' búdeš', no et' ne zaxóčeš'.

(2a) You'll live, but you won't feel much like fucking.

Sentence (2) is a phrase used to describe labor camp conditions to in-
coming prisoners

(3) Ja vas búdu káždy den' vot tak et'. Togdá naúčites' xodít'
stróju.

(3a) I'll ride you fuckers like this every day until you learn
how to march.

Sentence (1) can be used as an adjective with expletive force, but
it occurs uninflected. Sentence (1) would have to be entered in the lexicon
as an idiomatic entry. A general syntactic rule prevents the affixation of
inflectional desinences onto parenthetically used noun-phrases and sentences:

(4) Peredáj ëb tvojú mat' sol'.

(4a) Pass the fucking salt.

Note the following use of the true imperative:

(5) Ebí svojú, dešévle výidet.

(5a) Fuck your own (woman); you'll come out cheaper.

The reflexive form of the verb may be a reciprocal verb, in which
case it could have the underlying representation similar to the verb *fuck*
in English, as in *John and Mary were fucking* (see Quang 1968:2). As far
as we know, *ebát'* does not allow a female subject where the subject is
semantically the actor, but a NP referring to a female patient may be pro-
moted to the subject as in (6):

(6) Ebítes-ménee, akurátnej.

(6a) Fuck less often, but do it right.

where the verb is plural referring to a plural subject, presumably a male
and a female; the subject of an imperative is normally deleted. On the
other hand the reflexive form of the verb may be an intransitive verb with
the meaning 'to tinker with, mess around, screw around, or fuck around'.
The parallel here between Russian and English is interesting:

(7) Célyj den' s motórom ebús', a on xúja ne zabótitsja.

(7a) I've been fucking around with this motor all day, but it
won't start for shit.

The translation of *xúja* is figurative; literally *xuj* means 'cock, penis',
but it is used here in the genitive case and is roughly equivalent to the
English expression 'for shit', which is also interpreted figuratively in
English.

There are two momentary forms of the verb *ebát'*; one of them has the literal meaning 'to fuck once' (with one stroke?); it may also mean 'to strike with great force':

> (8) Egó tak vzrývom ebanúlo, čto on métrov pjat' letál.

> (8a) He caught such a fucking blow, that he flew about 15 feet (five meters).

The other verb, ëbnut',[5] means 'strike, hit, bang' (once):

> (9) On kak egó ëbnul po mórde, tak on i s kátišek dolój.

> (9a) He knocked him in the kisser so hard, that he knocked him off his pins.

3. Derivatives of the verb ebát'

There are several interesting derivatives derived from ebát'. The adjective ëbanyj is a simple derivative formed with the adjectival suffix /in/: /éb+ō+in/. The short forms ebën, ebén are derived from the non-thematic stem /eb/. The long-form adjective appears at first to be an attributively used participle, but this is not correct since /n/ does occur geminated in the surface structure; the attributive participle should be *ebannyj, but the form is not attested. Ëbanyj is an adjective of abuse and is used as an intensive form in the sense of 'absolute, downright'. In some contexts it loses all its meaning and serves as verbal spice similar to bloody or fucking in English. Although the two short forms often occur with v rot 'into the mouth', it occurs in the long form normally:

> (10) Èj, ty ëbanaja v rot bljad'.

> (10a) Hey, you cocksucking whore.

Other expressions include

> (11) Idí k ëbanoj máteri.

Sentence (11) is a very strong expletive approximately equivalent to English

> (1a) Go fuck yourself.

literally translated (11) means

> (11b) Go to your fucking mother.

> (12) Èj, ty žopoliz ëbanyj.

> (12a) Hey, you fucking ass-kisser.

Eblívyj 'liking to fuck' is derived from the verb stem /eb/ plus the adjective forming suffix /liu/; the adjective normally refers to a woman:

(13) Nu už takój eblívoj báby i svet ne vídel otrodjás'.

(13a) The world has never seen a woman who likes to fuck as she does.

The noun ëbar' refers to a man whose chief aim is sexual intercourse; or to a man who is sexually intimate with a woman other than his wife:

(14) Gladí-ka, éjnyj ëbar' pošël.

(14a) Look, the guy who fucks her has come.

Ejnyj ëbar' literally translates as 'her fucker'. The noun ebún has the same meaning as ëbar' in the first sense. Ebálo is an obscenity derived from /eb+ó´/ meaning 'mouth':

(15) Zakrój ebálo.

(15a) Shut your fucking mouth.

Ebálnik , which is derived from ebálo, means 'face' or sometimes 'nose'. Ebatórija is slang for difficult laborious work. The noun ebljá means literally fucking; otherwise it refers to a poorly organized, senseless work:

(16) Na sovétskix kurórtax byvájut mnógie žëny bez mužéj, i mužjá bez žën, no vsë ravnó, splošnaja ebljá tam.

(16a) At Soviet vacation resorts there are a lot of wives without husbands, and husbands without wives, but just the same there is fucking all over the place.

(17) V étom učreždénii zanimájutsja ne rabótoj a ebléj.

(17a) In this office they don't do any work, just a lot of fucking around.

(18) A načálas' ebljá s pljáskoj.

(18a) And then a fucking hullaballoo broke loose.

NOTES

[1] Forms are either cited in transliteration in italics, or they are cited in systematic phonemes by enclosing them in slashes (see note 3). The former is used when the citation of a form in systematic phonemes is not clear in the particular context in which it is used. The concept and description of the thematic suffix in Russian is discussed in DeArmond (1968). For an alternate description of the structure of the verb stem, see Micklesen (1970). The two analyses are compared and contrasted in DeArmond (forthcoming).

[2] The forms in italics referring to thematic suffixes are based on Jakobson's (1948) description and analysis of the Russian verb.

[3] Keeping with the convention of using slashes for underlying phonemic representations, and square brackets '[]' for phonological forms after a rule has occured (Harms 1968:2), we use a phonological alphabet which is nearly standard in Russian linguistics, but we do not make use of an alphabet such as the phonetically detailed I.P.A., since a phonetic description of Russian is beyond the scope of this paper.

[4] We use the term non-thematic to describe the class of Russian verbs with no thematic suffix, as opposed to athematic, because the latter term has traditionally been used to describe the extremely small class of verbs in the Slavic languages which do not have a thematic suffix and occur without a present tense suffix; there are two such verbs in Russian: dam, /dōd+m/ 'I will give', and em, /ēd+m/ 'I am eating', but idú, /īd+e+m/ 'I am going'.

[5] Stankiewicz (1962:18) mentions that Colloquial Russian has an unproductive category of expressive verbs with the suffix anu; since ebanút' is the only one of the two so paired verbs which literally means 'to fuck', it appears that these two momentary verbs do not follow the normal pattern in Russian.

REFERENCES

Chomsky, Noam, and Morris Halle. (1968) *The Sound Pattern of English*. New York: Harper & Row.

DeArmond, Richard C. (1968) *Deverbal and Deadjectival Verb Derivation in English and Russian*. Unpublished Ph.D. thesis, University of Chicago.

DeArmond, Richard C. (1969) The concept of word derivation. *Lingua* 22:329-61.

DeArmond, Richard C. (forthcoming) The derivational phonology of the Ukrainian verb.

Ferrell, J. (1956) On the differentiation of participles from deverbal adjectives arising from former participles. *Festschrift für Max Vasmer*, 147-50. Wiesbaden: Otto Harrasowitz.

Flier, Michael S. (1970) On the source of derived imperfectives in Russian. In D. Worth (ed.), *The Slavic Word*. The Hague: Mouton & Co.

Foo, Yuck. (1970) A selectional restriction involving pronoun choice. In the present volume.

Harms, Robert T. (1968) *Introduction to Phonological Theory*. Englewood Cliffs, N.J.: Prentice-Hall.

Halle, Morris. (1959) *The Sound Pattern of Russian*. The Hague: Mouton & Co.

Halle, Morris. (1963) O pravilax russkogo sprjažnenie. *American Contributions to the Fifth International Congress of Slavists*,113-32. The Hague: Mouton & Co.

Jakobson, Roman. (1932) Zur Sktruktur des russischen Verbums. *Charisteria Guilelmo Mathesio Quinquageneria*, 74-84. Prague: Sumptibus "Pražský lingvistický kroužek."

Jakobson, Roman. (1948) Russian conjugation. *Word* 4:155-67.

Jakobson, Roman. (1957) Shifters, verbal categories, and the Russian verb. Unpublished manuscript to appear in Roman Jakobson, *Selected Writings, II: Words and Language*. The Hague: Mouton & Co. (in press).

Lightner, Theodore M. (1963a) Remarks on the morphophonemic component of Russian. *Quarterly Progress Report (QPR)* 9:193-99. (Massachusetts Institute of Technology, Research Laboratory of Electronics.)

Lightner, Theodore M. (1963b) Nasal dipthongs in Russian. *QPR* 70:297-98.

Lightner, Theodore M. (1963c) Reduction of long 'i' in the Russian imperative, infinitive, and two singular morphemes. *QPR* 71:325-26.

Lightner, Theodore M. (1967) On the phonology of Russian conjugation. *Linguistics* 35:35-55.

Lightner, Theodore M. (1968) On the use of minor rules in Russian phonology. *Journal of Linguistics* 4:69-73.

Lopatin, V. V. (1966) Adjektivacija pričasij v ee otnošenii k slovoobrazovaniu. *Voprosy Jazykoznania* 55:37-47.

McCawley, James D. (1968a) Concerning the base component in a transform ational grammar. *Foundations of Language* 4:243-69.

McCawley, James D. (1968b) The role of semantics in a grammar. In E. Bach and R. Harms, (eds.), *Universals in Linguistic Theory*. New York: Holt, Rinehart & Winston. 125-70.

Micklesen, L.R. (1970) The structure of the Russian verb stems. In D. Worth (ed.), *The Slavic Word*. The Hague: Mouton & Co.

Quang, P. D. (1966) English sentences without overt grammatical subject. In the present volume.

Quang, P. D. (1968) A note on conjoined noun phrases. In the present volume.

Stankiewicz, Edward. (1962) The interdependence of paradigmatic and derivational patterns. *Word* 18:1-22.

A GENERATIVE PHONOLOGY OF YAKYAK

WM. K. RILEY
Georgetown University

Yakyak was a highly deflected language spoken by a small band of nomadic beings in the Mojave Desert toward the end of the last century. The band consisted of one old Indian man, his burro, and a number of desert rats and lizards who followed the old man in a close symbiotic relationship. A filling station attendant who had spoken to people who has heard the old Indian provided much of my information on Yakyak. Other data came from written materials in the form of two or three grocery lists and recordings of obscene stories reputed to have been those of the Yakyak speaker.

Since the only known speaker of Yakyak has been deceased for over a half century, I think I can say without fear of contradiction that the Yakyak vowel system was highly unnatural. (Or perhaps current formulations of the concept of naturalness are in error.) It appears to have had some processes of sound change operating which were very much like certain modern Chinese children's speech, (personal communication, Mao Tse Tung).

Specifically, Yakyak has a two-vowel system consisting of a low front rounded vowel, [œ], and a high back unrounded vowel, [ɯ]. These two vowels shared an allophone, [ɯ̥], which is a voiceless labio-dental nasal consonant. Since both of the other consonants of the language were also voiceless, the Yakyak speaker seldom seemed to be saying anything at all, and was only rarely observed to speak this intriguing language.

With regard to the vowel system, the best first approximation to a description would seem to include an alpha-switching rule such as the following (irrelevant facts omitted for simplification, such as third-formant location, for which see below):

$$V \rightarrow \begin{pmatrix} {}_{\cdot}w^{\wedge} \\ {}_{\Lambda}w^{>} \\ \Lambda w \end{pmatrix} \Big/ \#\# \underline{\hspace{1cm}} {}^{\infty}[\ CCCC({}^{\beta}\#*)]^{\ell} \Big\} \Big) \ ]]\ \#\#$$

$$\left\{ \begin{array}{c} \Lambda w^{\langle} \\ œ^{\wedge} \\ œ \end{array} \right.$$

$/ \oplus /$

$[\ddot{œ}]$

NP   NP

Conditions: α and β are never less than each other, and the height of the first formant of the second from the last vowel in the final or initial syllable (unless these are the same) correlates with the Dow-Laird Military-Industrial averages for June, 1968.

Anyway the rule looks something like the above, and has the effect of replacing any given vowel. X-ray data of a subject pronouncing several (two) Yakyak words reveals the inherent phonetic content of the underlying vowel system. Close examination of the X-rays shows a very definite lowering of the third formant in anticipation of fortis voicing as the drill contacts the right rear molar, and there is a small cavity in the adjacent

109

wisdom tooth.

It should be obvious that the findings of this study effectively refute both the Haskins Motor Theory of Perception and the Ding-Dong Theory of the origin of language. Little else remains to be done.

NOTE

* Phonemic notation is used here instead of distinctive features, since Yakyak is not only not distinctive, but also essentially featureless.

II. PORNOLINGUISTICS AND SCATOLINGUISTICS

D. Metapornolinguistics

CONJUNCTIVE ORDERING

E. Clifton Gamahuche

The following note lays down a definitive order for a number of rules that have been discussed in so-called generative[1] grammar. There has been an astonishing amount of disagreement among otherwise reputable scholars on this childishly simple question of rule ordering. There is only one conceivable ordering which will yield maximal satisfaction. I will refer to this ordering as <u>conjunctive</u> ordering.

1.   In conjunctive ordering, at some time after <u>Aux Attraction</u>, <u>Copula Agreement</u> may take place. Then, after (optional) <u>Scrambling</u>, it is obligatory that <u>Subject Raising</u>, and other expansion rules, occur. After the maximal strip of the adverb has been obtained, <u>Adverb Lowering</u> will naturally take place, closely followed by <u>Swooping</u>. Since <u>Scrambling</u> is an anywhere rule, more of it may be in order; do not hesitate.

Thus far we have not endeavored to attain the goal of observational adequacy, for which some showier rules may be employed. I refer of course to <u>Subject-Verb Inversion</u>. <u>Scrambling</u> will almost certainly recur, and soon, too soon, <u>Affix Hopping</u> will obligatorily ensue.

Pausing briefly, to catch our breath before the next block of rules, we may wish to limit our generative capacity by imposing an output condition. If so, we will undergo <u>Neg Placement</u>. But conjunctive ordering without this device is often preferred.

We are now ready for <u>Gapping</u>! Making sure that all conditions on the input configuration for this next, crucial, rule are met, we embark upon the glorious rule of <u>There Insertion</u>. <u>Clefting</u> follows. More <u>Scrambling</u>. If <u>Extraposition</u> is desired, a variety of rules suggest themselves, such as <u>Right Dislocation</u> and <u>Left Dislocation</u>, and even, for advanced students, <u>Verb Final</u>.[2]

Now is no time for the <u>Passive</u>! <u>Conjunct Movement</u> must take place and <u>Tough Movement</u> too! The next two rules are ordered so closely that many scholars regard them as simultaneous: <u>Vocative Formation</u> and then the justly celebrated <u>Particle Movement</u>.

Alas, the time will come for <u>Conjunction Reduction</u>. If there has been no <u>Neg Placement</u>, or if this process has been succeeded by <u>Neg Hopping</u>, <u>Sluicing</u> may be advisable, in order to ensure <u>Tense Prevention</u>.

I can see no justification for Chomsky's suggested constraint[3] that would prohibit the insertion of material into an already processed clause, so I see no reason (unless <u>Performative Deletion</u> has

applied) for not recycling through the greater part of the
list of rules above -- although before the first rules, Do Support
may be necessary.

Copula Agreement will be required again. In its absence, there
is but one possible rule: Reflexivization.

NOTES

[1] A total misnomer, as the discussion of Neg Placement below shows
conclusively.

[2] Some scholars have suggested that this is an appropriate place
in the ordering for Pruning. I do not even understand their
suggestion, I regret to say.

[3] *Aspects of the Theory of Syntax*, M.I.T. Press, 1965, p. 146.

III. WHIMSY I

LANGUAGE

JOURNAL OF THE DEBATING

SOCIETY OF AMERICA

[Communicated by Carolyn Killean, George Lakoff,
Robin Lakoff, Michael O'Malley, and Lester Rice]

Morris Halle: #

-cons	+cons	#	+cons	-cons	+cons	+cons	+cons
+voc	-voc		-comp	+voc	-voc	-voc	+voc
-diff	-comp		-grav	+diff	-comp	-comp	-flat
+comp	-grav		-int	-comp	+grav	+grav	
+grav	+int		+tens	+grav	+int	+int	
-tens	+nas		+strd	-tens	+nas	+tens	
+flat				-flat		-nas	
						-strd	

(title to be continued on pp. 2-4)

118

Publications Received:
    Bloch, Stockwell and Carroll: Prolegomena to Aspects of the Theory
        of Categories of Unified Relations of Structural Behavior of
        Syntactic Networks
    Z. Harris: Studies Presented to N. Chomsky on the Occasion of his
        Bar Mitzvah
    Yngve: A Field Guide to Massachusetts Trees
    J. McCawley: Happiness is a Pre-Publication Copy

Publications to be Received:
    Chomsky and Halle: The Sound Pattern of English
    Lamb: The Semantic Structure of Sememics
    U.S.Rubber: External Reconstruction of a Proto-Ladefoged

MAXEME'S: THE LINGUIST'S RESTAURANT

RICHARD CARTER, JEFFREY GRUBER, GEORGE LAKOFF,
ROBIN LAKOFF, and JOHN ROBERT ROSS

MENYUK

HORS d'OEUVRES

Fruit Joos
Martineted Herring
Hummingboldt's Tongue
Yuan Ren Chaoder

Escarghosh
Raw Oysterlitz
New Mock Turtle Soup
Sprachgefühlte Fish

ANTIPOSTAL

Sphocketti and Meatballs

Mackayroni

ENTRÉES (À LA CARTER)

Sapirribs
Lakoff Lamb
Pottroast

Sole Saporta
Corned Beef Hodge
Boiled Hallebutt

INTERNATIONAL CUISINE

Chom Skuey
Chao Mein
Sukijakobson
Yukisaki
Enchiladefoged

Haasenpfeffer
Verner Schnitzel
Labov Bourguignon
Wells Rarebit

CONDIMENTS

Katzup
Horswadesh
Salt and Peipper

Hallidaise Sauce
Rulon Welish

GARVIN VEGETABLES

McCawleyflower
Klima Beans
Mashed Poteeters
Asapiragus
Cornyn the Cob

Troubeetskoy
Kiparsley
Longokra
Sledduce
Bloch-eyed Peas

FROM OUR GRILL AND TWADDELLICATESSEN

Hampburgers
Frankfodors
Chile con Charney
Grilled Lees Sandivič
Lotz and Bagels

Peanut Butter and Zellig
  Sandivič
Hoijered Boijeled Eggs
Cold Katz

PASTRIES

Grimm Crackers
Hall Wheat Bread
E. Wayles Brownies

Humboldt Pie
Lehmann Meringue P.I.E.
Blochlava

DESSERTS

Pāṇini Split
Charles Freeze
Ice Cream Kuno

Bached Alisker
Idiot's Delightner
Strawberry Shortquirk

FRUITS

Grapes of Kurath
Applesaussure
Aprikoutsoudas

Kumkatz
Rhubarbara
Pineapplegate

BEVER-AGES

Rheinweinreich
Bierwisch an Egg in It
Martinet
Levin Ordinaire
Soda Bopp

Puhveltine
Lemonida
Bonfan Tea
Lukoffee
Schrammpagne

BREAKFAST DISHES

Rice Vacheks
Raisin Braine
Corn Flakoffs
Oatmeillet
Cream of Whitney

Pengcakes
Whorfles
Toast and Hahney or
  Marmeladefoged
Schrammbled Eggs

A CONCISE HISTORY OF MODERN ART[*]

FOM POP
University of Alberta

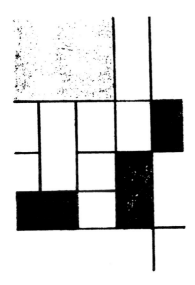

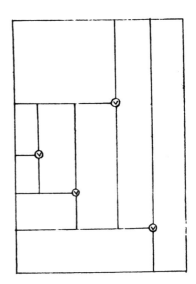

"STILL LIFE WITH COW"

*Piet Mondrian

"ALL THIS FRESH MILK ON THE TABLE"

Charles Hockett

[*] For concision, the accompanying text has been transformed according to the following rule:

$$S \rightarrow \emptyset \; / \; \underline{\qquad}$$

122

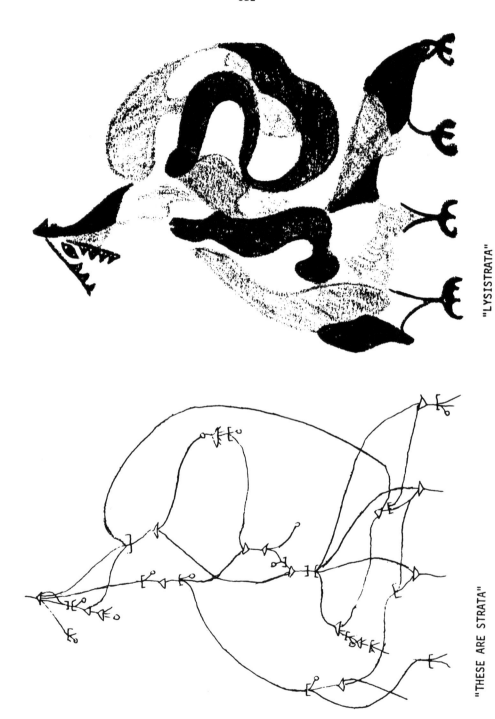

"LYSISTRATA"　　*Pablo Picasso

"THESE ARE STRATA"　　Sidney Lamb

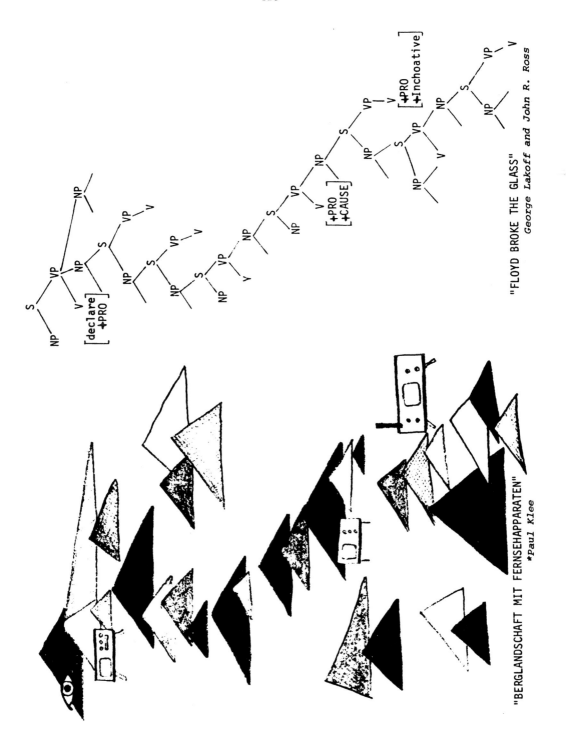

"FLOYD BROKE THE GLASS"
George Lakoff and John R. Ross

"BERGLANDSCHAFT MIT FERNSEHAPPARATEN"
*Paul Klee

GLOSSARY OF LINGUISTIC TERMINOLOGY

*U. PANI SHAD et alii**
University of Massachusetts et alibi

Rhotacirrm
Ableut
Haplogy
Pocopy
Syncpy
Metasethis
Gemminnattionn
Reduduplication
Assimilassion
nansal infinx
Holtzmann's Laggus
Ghrassmann's Lhaw
Krimm's Law
Umläut
Auslautsverhärtunk [= Terminal devoicink]
sechont sount shipftz
athemtic
Sprossevokal
epenethesis
savarabhakati
sfiranthization
frixaþiv
Breachung
Diaphthoungiazaytion
Zro Grde [= Schwnd Stfe]
Diθsimilation
Vowol harmonu
compênstry lêngthning
finix

* Alli sunt: Gary D. Bevington, James E. Cathey,
Richard Demers, E. W. Y. Lemon, Quang P. D.
(visiting gloss).

A SUPPLEMENTARY GLOSSARY OF LINGUISTIC TERMINOLOGY[1]

U BAL SHADA ZWEL et alii
University of Alberta et alibi

Apfrication

Assililation[1]

Dissimulation[2]

Dedasalization

Deladialization

Glo'alization

Haspiration

Nanalization

Palatialization

Tefocalization

Trieiphthuoungization[3]

Vogalization

Wabiawization

Fall Sandhi

In^{to}^{na}t$_i$$_{on}$

Anaphoŝtre

Anapityxis

Apocop[4]

Apopheny[5]

Dittolology[6]

Ecthlips

Epithesisk

Hypercoristikins

Hyserthepis[7]

Paragogyn

Pheresis

Polnogolosie

Přehléska

Sampṛsarana

Ellpsis

Pleonastic Perissological Tautology

NOTES

[1] viz., to U Pani Shad (1971; henceforth ŪPS). The lists originally repeated each other in some particulars; the present authors have made the necessary omssions to avoid dupliplication.

[2] cp. ŪPS: "Assimilassion" and "Diθsimilation": there is apparently a terminological conflict here.

[3] cp. ŪPS: "Diaphthoungiazaytion".

[4] cp. ŪPS: "Pocopy". We take issue with ŪPS here; they are obviously confusing *apocop* and *pheresis*.

127

[5] cp. ŪPS: "Ableut".

[6] cp. ŪPS: "Reduduplication".

[7] cp. ŪPS: "Metasethis". *Hyserthepis* is thus defined as metasethis at a coblideranse dincaste; emplaxes of hyserthepis are angom the stom ntogec antumergs anstaig the thyore of laduagr tonephic ngache.

REFERENCE

Shad, U Pani et alii. (1971) Glossary of linguistic terminology. In the present volume.

THE LINGUIST'S SONGBOOK
(SING A LANGUAGE MITCH)

RICHARD CARTER, GEORGE LAKOFF,
ROBIN LAKOFF, and JOHN ROBERT ROSS

ANTHEMS AND HYMNS

The Transformationale
The DuMarsaillaise
The NP Star Spangled Banner
  (Oh see if you can say...)
Whorf We Go, Into the Wild
  Blue Yonder
Huichol Overcome
Onward Chretien Soldiers

ROCK 'N' ROLL

I Want to Hold Your Hamp
Olney You
We Can Quirk It Out

FEATURED HITS

Will You Still Be Minus?
Compact To Sorrento
The Consonantal
I Velar Song Comin' On
I Get a Click Out of You
The Trill Is Gone
Once In Love With Angma

SHOW TUNES

Geis and Dolls
Anything Ghosh
Stormy Bever
I've Grown Accustomed to Your Base
I Love Harris in the Stringtime
Ullmann River
The Lady Is a Hamp

BERBERSHOP BALLADS

Roll Out the Bar-Hillel
Noam But You
Kruisinga Down the River
Come Josephine in My Turing
  Machine

WÖLCK SONGS

Old Black Joos
Little White Lees
This Lunt is My Lunt
Hił Got the Whole World
  In His Hamp
The Old Grammaire, She
  Ain't What She Used to Be
Where Have All the Fowlers Gone?
Frère Schachter
Emeneauld Cowhand
Oh Dear, Watkins Delattre Be?
We Are Motsching to Praetoria

CLASSICS

Afternoon of a Phone
Sapir Gynt Suite
Grand Kenyon Sweet
Matthews der Maler
Curmen

HALLIDAY SONGS

O Stammenbaum
The Firth Noel
Silent Nida, Holy Nida
Here Comes Teeter Cottontail
Deck the Halls!

STANDARDS

Swadesh This Thing Called Love?
Let McCawleyou Sweetheart
I've Got De Rijk to Sing the Blues
All Alone By the Allophone
Postal-Packin' Momma
Isn't It Semantic?
That's a Mora!
That Old Bloch Magic
Never on Sandhi
I'm Guna Sit Right Down and Write
    Myself a Letter
Menomini Done Tole Me
Thanks Fodor Memory

Arrivederci Roman
How Deep Is the Notion?
Alexander's Ragtime Bantu
The Darktown Structure Ball
When I'm McCawleying You
Come Xhosa to Me
It Haj to Be You
Honeycycle Rose
Birwisched, Bothered, and
    Bewildered
Zipf a Dee Doo Dah
Bach to Bach, Bally to Bally
I Meillet Be Wang

IV. PARODY AND BURLESQUE I: INSIDE TG GRAMMAR

ON NOTATIONAL CONVENTIONS:
NEW EVIDENCE FROM THE FIELD

EBBING CRAFT
Hamtramck School for Girls

0.   During the summer of 1967 a grant from the National Aeronautics
and Space Administration, supplemented by a modest subvention from
the American Nazi Party, enabled the author to pursue intensive informant
work with the last known speaker of the Urbanan language, the only reported
member of the Urbanan family of languages, the wider linguistic affinities
of which are still obscure.[1] Until the author's foray into the field, the
language was but poorly described, although it has often been cited (for
example, by Pie 1948) as a language with extensive consonant clustering.
In fact, the language exhibits a number of phonological, morphological, and
semantic peculiarities, some of which appear to be unique among the world's
languages. The importance of Amerindian field work, especially in the
many rapidly disappearing stocks, could hardly be more dramatically under-
lined.[2]

In the sections to follow we shall take up in order (a) the circumstances surrounding the field work, (b) certain difficulties that arise
in the phonemic analysis of Urbanan, and (c) the elegant solution of these
difficulties in the framework proposed in the long-awaited *Sound Pattern
of Pig Latin* by Chumsky and Hella. In this last section we shall demonstrate that the evidence from Urbanan provides strong empirical support
for a number of notational conventions proposed in that work. A table
contains nominal forms illustrating the phenomena discussed in the main
body of the text.[3]

1.   The informant was Mrs. Bpétí Bpúk,[4] an imposing but gracious lady
of 94, and the last remnant of the once-proud U[5] nation. Mrs. Bpúk
and the author met for approximately eight hours of elicitation per day,
every day for fourteen weeks, in the informant's hogan adjacent to the
University of Illinois Assembly Hall. Elicitation proceeded at a rather
slow pace, for three reasons: (a) the right-hand side of Mrs. Bpúk's body
was completely paralyzed; (b) it had been 26 years since Mrs. Bpúk had
attempted conversation in U, the penultimate speaker of U, her fourth hus-
band, Kwaŋ Dóŋ,[6] having been swept away in an avalanche in the "fearsome
spring" of 1941; and (c) Mrs. Bpúk suffered, periodically, from various
quaint delusions[7] which sometimes affected her utility as an informant.

Despite these various difficulties, the writer succeeded in drawing
forth from Mrs. Bpúk material sufficient to clarify the principal phonological and morphological features of U. Moreover, the informant was able
to supply a considerable amount of material in a hitherto unreported dia--
lect of U, Rantoulish, which differs from U in three minor respects -- the
analogical extension of the vocative absolute construction, the elimination
of pronouns in favor of numerical indices, and the addition of two rules
to the end of the phonological component of U.[8] Shortly after the informant
sessions ended, Mrs. Bpúk was killed in a freak surfing accident. It is to
the memory of that brave woman that this paper is dedicated.

2.   Most prominent among the phonological characteristics of U are the clustering of consonants already noted, extensive nasalization of vowels, subtle alternations in pitch, and a delicate pattern of alternation between *i* and *e* on one hand, *u* and *o* on the other. Among the morphological properties of the language, notable are the unmarked[9] character of the Accusative Plural and the complete absence of number distinctions in the Nominative case.[10] The brevity of many highly technical, presumably borrowed, vocabulary items, the complexity of numerous quite common, presumably native, lexical entries, and the extraordinary range of cultures represented in what the informant consistently identified as ordinary unaffected speech constitute the most irravelable riddles for the future U lexicologist.[11] Thus, the existence of two monosyllabic roots with identical realization **pé** in the Accusative Plural, one meaning 'noun', the other 'verb', is noteworthy,[12] as are the length of the nursery words for 'mother' (Acc. Pl. *zúvóná*) and 'father' (Acc. Pl. *loxúgk*)[13] and the range of concepts represented by the Acc. Pl. forms *é* 'horseshoe', *ó* 'prime minister', *ó* 'DNA', and *á* 'bean thread', or even *lema* 'poi jar' and *ómne* 'monorail'.[14]

We now turn directly to the phonological system of U. U has five vowels, *i e a o u*, each of which may be either oral or nasalized, and each of which may occur with either low pitch or high pitch; there is thus a total of 20 phonetically distinct vowels, all of which, as it turns out, are also phonemically distinct.[15] Relevant forms, all nouns in the Acc. Pl. as usual,[16] follow:

(a) *kím* 'four of hearts'; *kim* 'radish heart'; *kem* 'middle toe'; *kám* 'quiet'; *kam* 'salt cellar'; *kóm* 'shot to side pocket'; *kom* 'rapist'; *kúm* 'cigarette'; *kum* 'flatiron'; *kém* 'uvula'.

(b) *úzíŋ* 'fishhook'; *úzĩn* 'self-defrosting refrigerator' and ɣ*úzĩn* 'taro'; *úzĩn* 'perfidy' and *kúzĩn* 'thresher'; *kuzin* 'reindeer harness'.

Forms analogous to the (b) series can be found for the remaining four vowels.

The U consonant system, *p t k b d g f s x v z ɣ m n ŋ l*, requires little comment. All 16 consonants contrast in word-final position in monosyllabic nouns:[17]

káp 'fuzz'; *kát* 'chaise longue'; *kák* 'penis (of one's own)'; *káb* 'rind'; *kád* 'haddock'; *kág* 'depersonalized one'; *káf* 'husky voice'; *kás* 'reason'; *káx* 'penis (of another)'; *káv* 'inscription'; *káz* 'excuse'; *káɣ* 'wheel'; *kám* 'quiet'; *kán* 'resort'; *káŋ* 'ape'; *kál* 'telephone message'.

Both vowel clusters and consonant clusters occur, the former much less frequently than the latter; but all two-vowel sequences except those with the pitch pattern low-high are attested. Some examples are included in the table below. There are essentially no constraints upon the occurence of consonants, singly or in clusters, except that *f s x b d g* do not appear in word-initial position. It is possible to contemplate alternative phonemicizations in which various consonant clusters are treated as unit phonemes (e.g., *bp, dt, gk, vf, zs, ɣx* might be transcribed as half-

voiced consonants B, D, G, V, Z, γ, respectively), but these phonemicizations are all mechanically interconvertible; in accordance with the considerations of note 15 above, we choose the phonetically most natural pho-
nemicization, in which clusters are treated as clusters, with no hocus-
pocus.[18]

3.   The morphophonemics of U would indeed do credit to any of the better-
described exotic languages. The bold strokes of this intricate linguistic portrait have already been sketched -- the magnificent undulation
of the tonal system as it flows through the nominal paradigm, the rough
banishment of f s x b d g when they dare to stand before the gate of the
word, the lambent play of vowel qualities as i and e, u and o, flash and
blend in root and prefix both, the nasal murmurings that glide from point
to point, all in harmony with the most minute adjustments in the signifi-
cations of those consummate aesthetic objects which we linguists have come
to know, so harshly, as utterances. Let us delve further into these
mysteries, so as to attain to a transcendental comprehension of the inner
harmony and creativity of this language.

This comprehension is to be reached through the notational conventions of the *Sound Pattern of Pig Latin*, a manuscript of which was made
available[19] to the writer during the period of elicitation. Contemplate
the forms in the table below. As in the forms already cited, unmarked
vowels have low pitch, and accented vowels have high pitch. The problem
is to account for all alternations, and to account for all pitches.

		Acc.pl.	$\begin{Bmatrix}\text{Voc}\\\text{Acc}\end{Bmatrix}$sg.	Nom.$\begin{Bmatrix}\text{sg.}\\\text{pl.}\end{Bmatrix}$	Voc.pl.	Gloss
I.	1.	é	óé	pée	láé	horseshoe
	2.	é	óí	péi	láí	fireplug
	3.	pé	upé	pípẽ	lapẽ́	noun
	4.	pé	pé	pípĭ	lapĭ́	verb
	5.	ké	oké	pékẽ	lakẽ́	university
	6.	ké	okí	pékĭ	lakĭ́	left hind leg of a ram
II.	1.	kúm	okúm	píkŭm	lakŭ́m	cigarette
	2.	kum	úfkŭm	pífn̥um	láfn̥um	flatiron
	3.	é	úmé	pímĭ	lámĭ	steamship
	4.	é	úmé	pímẽ	lámẽ́	copulation
	5.	évĭ́	úné é	píxŭle	lánẽ́vé	hip
	6.	úlẽ	axúne	píxŭle	laxŭ́le	metaphor
	7.	ápã	uxáma	píxãpa	laxápa	charisma
	8.	lema	úxlẽpa	píxnepa	láxnepa	poi jar
	9.	ómne	ufómte	pífõmte	lafõmte	monorail
III.	1.	áf	únáf	pínãf	lánãf	vampire bat
	2.	óŋ	usóŋ	písõŋ	lasǫ̃ŋ	art exhibit
	3.	ó	úbó	píbŭ	lábŭ	prime minister
	4.	ó	oxú	péxŭ	laxŭ́	DNA
	5.	á	ógá	pégã	lágã́	bean thread
	6.	γé	óγé	péγẽ	láγẽ́	rejection
	7.	íbĭd	úgímíd	pígĭbid	lágĭbĭd	penguin
	8.	zéγĭg	úzéγíg	pízĭγeg	lázĭγég	footnote

Acc. pl.	{Voc./Acc.} sg.	Nom. {sg./pl.}	Voc.pl.	Gloss
IV. 1. ptis	úptĩs	p̃ipnis	lápnis	giant sea turtle
2. akóṇa	oakúga	péaṇoga	láaṇ́ógá	enemy of an in-law
3. tfeɣunk	útfeɣunk	p̃ítfeɣunk	látf̧eɣunk	thumb(obscene)
4. zásn	úzást	p̃ízàst	lázàst	debutante
5. ɣóbṇó	uyomtó	p̃íɣõbto	laɣõbtó	infant
6. lox̧ugk	uloxógk	p̃ílũxogk	lalũxógk	father
7. oxũg	udoxúg	p̃ídũxug	ladũxúg	flea(on another)
VV. 1. zúvóná	úzúvóná	p̃ízũvona	lázũvóná	mother
2. limpéɣmos	udlĩmpéɣmos	p̃ídnimpeɣmos	ladnimpéɣmos	house
3. ovĩtó	uṇovitó	p̃íṇõvito	laṇ̃gvitó	giggle
4. tútĩpan	utúṇipan	p̃ítũtipan	latũtipan	thumb(polite)
5. uséne	uusēte	p̃íusete	lauséte	passion
VI. 1. kvoṇin	úkvõṇen	p̃íkvoṇin	lákvoṇin	pederast
2. kxoṇin	ókxũṇin	pékxoṇin	lákxoṇin	Peoria
3. pexģŋg	úsp̃íxeŋg	p̃ísmexeŋg	lásmexeŋg	licorice
4. zlpág	úzlmág	p̃íznpag	laznpág	flea(on oneself)

Let us begin with the simplest of the four morphophonemic processes illustrated in the data, the deletion of word-initial *f s x b d g m n ŋ*. That the process is a deletion and not a morpheme structure condition is apparent from the alternations above; in these forms all case-number combinations other than the Acc. Pl. (that is, all prefixed forms) contain throughout one of these consonants, which is lacking in the Acc. Pl. form. The relevant forms are II-2, II-9; III-2, VI-3; II-6, II-7, II-8, III-4; III-3, IV-7, V-2; III-5, III-7; II-3, II-4; III-1; II-5, V-3. To formulate the rule we need a notational convention that treats the nine consonants under consideration as a natural class but excludes *v z ɣ p t k l*. The alpha-notation[20] captures this generalization in a most extraordinarily elegant way: the class of deletable segments is the class of [αcont, −αvoice] segments, that is, segments which are continuant and voiceless or noncontinuant and voiced. The rule is

$$(A) \quad \begin{vmatrix} \alpha\text{cont} \\ -\alpha\text{voice} \end{vmatrix} \rightarrow \emptyset \ / \ \# \underline{\hspace{1cm}}$$

Having solved the problem of initial consonants, we are now able to make an intelligent approach to the nasal-oral alternations in the vowels and consonants.[21] The explanation of these alternations lies in a type of phenomenon which, curiously enough, has remained unstudied, even unremarked upon, in over ten years of earth-shaking discoveries within the field of generative phonology. The phenomena in question are those which depend crucially upon the precise distance of a segment from the beginning (or end) of a word. Our present problem is only slightly complicated by the fact that the rule in question must be extrinsically ordered before Rule (A). The reader will quickly discern that if the initial consonants are restored to all roots exemplified in the data, then the prediction of nasal segments is simple: the fourth segment of the word is nasal (unless, of course, it is a continuant obstruent, the occurrence of nasal continuant obstruents being limited to infantile imitations of airplane engines). Some slight phonetic complexity is added by the fact that *n* is the nasalized version not only of *d* but also of *t* (cf., II-9) and *l* (cf., II-8), just as

m is the nasalized version of both b and p, and η of both g and k. The rule is

(B) $[+\text{seg}]$ $\rightarrow$ $[+\text{nas}]$ $/$ $\#$ $[+\text{seg}]_3^3$ ____ [22]

We next take up the prediction of pitch in Urbanan. In a taxonomic description of the language undertaken in the early months of elicitation, a handful of generalizations were appended to the phonemic description, which (as discussed in earlier sections) treated all pitch markings as phonemic. For example, the Nom.Sg.-Pl. form always has pitch on the initial syllable. Also, the Voc.-Acc.Sg. and the Voc.Pl. forms normally have the same pitch pattern, although there are some exceptions (e.g., IV-2 and VI-4). The observation that the pitch rule must be ordered after Rule (B) but before Rule (A) provides the key. With this ordering, it becomes crystal clear that the principles of high pitch prediction are the following: (a) If all consonants in a word, except perhaps for those in a word-final cluster, are voiced, all vowels have high pitch (cf., the Acc.Pl. forms in II-5, III-7, III-8, IV-5, V-1, the Voc.Pl. forms in III-6, IV-2, IV-4, and the Voc.-Acc.Sg. form in IV-4); (b) otherwise, if there is a vowel immediately following the first voiceless consonant in the word, that vowel has high pitch (cf., all Nom.Sg.-Pl. forms, and the Voc.Pl. forms in II-6, II-9, IV-5, IV-7, V-2, V-3, V-4, and VI-4); (c) otherwise, if the first vowel in a word is in word-initial position or is preceded by voiced consonants only, then that vowel has high pitch (cf., the Voc.Pl. forms in II-2, IV-1, and VI-3). An entirely equivalent formulation of these principles uses the fact that vowels are themselves voiced: (a) If there is a vowel following the first voiceless segment in a word, then it (and only it) has high pitch; (b) otherwise, all vowels (and only those vowels) preceded by a sequence of (zero or more) voiced segments extending back to the beginning of the word have high pitch (this clause combines clauses (a) and (c) of the previous formulation). In symbols,

$$\begin{bmatrix} +\text{voc} \\ -\text{cons} \end{bmatrix} \rightarrow [+\text{highpitch}] \quad / \left\{ \begin{array}{l} \# \ [+\text{voice}]_0 \ [-\text{voice}] \ \underline{\quad} \\ \# \ [+\text{voice}]_0 \ \underline{\quad} \end{array} \right\}$$

(using the convention that subrules abbreviated by subscripts are applied simultaneously and that subrules abbreviated by brackets apply in disjunctive order). A further notational convention leads to our final formulation of this rule:

(C) $\begin{bmatrix} +\text{voc} \\ -\text{cons} \end{bmatrix}$ $\rightarrow$ $[+\text{highpitch}]$ $/$ $\#$ $[+\text{voice}]_0$ $([-\text{voice}])$ ____

The absence of high pitch in II-2, as opposed to II-1, is explained by the fact that Rule (C) applies before Rule (A). The complex alternations of pitch in VI-4 are explained by the fact that Rule (C) applies after Rule (B), which has the (as it were, fortuitous) effect of replacing a voiceless stop by a voiced (nasal) one in the Voc.-Acc.Sg. form.

The reasoning behind the postulation of the fourth rule, which predicts all replacements of i by e and u by o, both in prefixes and in roots, is too lengthy to be exposed in full in the present discussion, although the reasoning is entirely of the same sort that led to the postulation of the preceding three rules. The most notable features of this rule are the way in which vacuous application of its subrules affects the interpretation of disjunctive ordering, and the remarkable formal similarity of the rule to the celebrated Pig Latin Maine Stress Rule formulated by Chumsky and Hella. The rule:

$$(D) \quad \begin{vmatrix} +voc \\ -cons \\ -nas \end{vmatrix} \rightarrow [-high] \ / \ \underline{\quad\quad} \ [-ant]_0 \ (\begin{vmatrix} +voc \\ -cons \\ -nas \end{vmatrix} \ \begin{vmatrix} +cons \\ -voc \end{vmatrix}_0)^1 \ \#$$

Two points must be stressed: First, the interpretation of the future anterior, by which the set of [-ant] segments in Urbanan consists of the velar consonants and all the vowels; second, the class of segments affected by the rule, which is the class of all oral vowels, not only the oral vowels *i* and *u*, so that the first subrule (with the extra syllable in the environment) will apply vacuously in many forms, thereby (by ordinary and now familiar conventions of disjunctive ordering) making the second subrule (without the extra syllable) inapplicable.[23] The first subrule calls for a final VC_0 syllable to be disregarded unless it (a) ends in more than one consonant (consider the forms in IV-6 as opposed to IV-7), or (b) contains a nasalized vowel (observe the forms in II-1 and II-2, for example). If the first subrule applies, any (oral) *i* or *u* in the penultimate or earlier, syllable is lowered so long as all consonants intervening between that vowel vowel and the final VC_0 syllable are velars. Of course, the rule applies vacuously to all occurrences of *é o a* in the appropriate environments. If this subrule applies, vacuously or otherwise, the second subrule does not apply; the forms in I, those in II-3 through II-8, and those in VI-1 and VI-2 illustrate some of the possibilities.

If the first subrule does not apply, either because no vowel satisfies the environmental conditions or because all vowels satisfying the conditions are nasalized, then the second subrule will apply -- to all oral vowels followed by sequences consisting entirely of vowels and velars terminating at the end of the word.

Rule (D) bears a considerable formal similarity to (and uses exactly the same number of feature specifications as) the Maine Stress Rule of Pig Latin, in a formulation of the latter rule which disregards many of the complexities of that problematic language:

$$(E) \quad \begin{bmatrix} +voc \\ -cons \end{bmatrix} \rightarrow [+stress] \ / \ \underline{\quad\quad} \ \begin{bmatrix} +cons \\ -voc \end{bmatrix}_0 \ (\begin{bmatrix} +voc \\ -cons \\ -tense \end{bmatrix} \ \begin{bmatrix} +cons \\ -voc \end{bmatrix}_0)^1 \ \#$$

The similarity is either entirely fortuitous or else speaks for a closer relation between Urbanan and Pig Latin that has ever been hypothesized before.

One final remark: The informant was able to supply a sufficient number of forms from the Rantoulish dialect of Urbanan to indicate that the phonology of Rantoulish is identical to that of (Classical) Urbanan, except that Rantoulish has achieved an almost perfect CVCV... pattern within the word, by means of two ordered rules, here presented informally:

$$(E) \quad C \rightarrow \emptyset \ / \ \#V_0CV_0(CV_0CV_0)_0 \ \underline{\quad\quad}$$

(F) $\emptyset \rightarrow z$ / V ____ V

The effect of Rule (E) is to reduce consonant clustering by the elimination of every other consonant, regardless of intervening vowel structure. The effect of Rule (F) is to eliminate all cases of vowel hiatus, both those original in Urbanan and those created by the Rantoulish Rule (E), by the insertion of a z. Curiously enough, this writer found it devilishly difficult to learn Rantoulish, although this observation is undoubtedly purely autobiographical.

NOTES

[1] Bluebird(1953c) postulates a relationship with Penutian; this identification rests, however, on observed similarities in less than ten percent of the items on an English-Urbanan word list collected in 1908 by a Decatur junior high school student visiting Urbana for a tour of the experimental soybean fields. Other affinities -- namely, with Dardic and Finno-Ugric -- have been suggested, but none is well supported. See Craft (1966) for a review of the evidence.

[2] See Latsop (1967) for a contrary, but rude, opinion and Pocketa-Queep (1966) for a crushing rejoinder.

[3] Extensive exemplification of Urbanan, in the form of transcriptions of Mrs. Bpûk's retelling of the classic Myth of the Hazelnut and the Henbane and of lengthy reminiscences of her early life, are in preparation. Their publication has been, unfortunately, delayed by legal difficulties associated with the nature of their content.

[4] Mrs. Bpûk's name constitutes an intriguing puzzle for Urbanan (U in the remainder of this work) etymologists. The name is thoroughly non-Urbanan (non-U in the remainder of this work), in that all other known U proper names are tetrasyllabic words referring to articles of clothing and in that the name contains otherwise disallowed occurrences of word-initial *bp*, contains unpredictable high pitches, contains unpredictable instances of *i* and *u*, and lacks expected nasal vowels and nasal consonants in certain positions. Gorge Coughlake (personal communication) has suggested that the name is a version of the American English proper name *Betty Boop*. Mrs. Bpûk's assertion that she was named after her paternal grandfather works against this hypothesis.

[5] For an explanation of this abbreviation, see the previous note.

[6] A Tlingit-Urbanan bilingual, reputed to have had a reading knowledge of Telugu and Old French, who made a tenuous living as a slag-picker along the Illinois Central railroad near Kankakee.

[7] One very frequent delusion, which never interfered with her ability to recall the forms and phrases of U, was that she spoke Crimean Gothic and that I was a Flemish traveller named Busbecq. In her less lucid moments she believed herself to be Tony Tillohosh, or that she was afflicted with a Boolean condition on analyzability.

[8] See Section 3 for a brief discussion of this last development.

[9] In the now well-known sense of the Camelot Round Table of Linguistics, adumbrated in von Humbert Humbert (1802), promulgated in Yarmulka (1917), and fully elaborated, without the earlier taxonomic bias, in the epochal Chumsky (1957).

[10] Since this article went to press, the eminent Sinologist Chu-Chin Chow has kindly informed me that Mandarin, too, lacks such distinctions.

[11] An interesting oddity is the occurrence of two words meaning 'thumb', one obscene, the other not. No such distinction is recognized in any of the languages cited in Merry Hausa's encyclopedic monograph on the subject (Hausa 1951) or in the Bluebird (1953a) addendum to it. As it happens, this writer was unable to determine the function of the thumb in U culture.

[12] And must have been troublesome to the native U grammarians, had there been any.

[13] But see the author's forthcoming 'Why zúvoná and loxúgk?' in the Proceedings of the XXth Interurban Conference on Onomastic Hygiene.

[14] We shall not lend credence to Sturdyvat's preposterous Urbano-Tektite Hypothesis by mentioning it in connection with these forms, which have so persistently and so tediously, as in Hen (1949), been offered as evidence in its favor.

[15] If the author interprets Pocketa-Queep (1958), Lamp (1964), and Glissando (1965) correctly, this result is in accordance with their hypothesis that phonemics is identical to phonetics, the famous "double articulation" theory of language. But Latsop (1967), in an extended criticism of these works, maintains that the Pocketa-Queep-Lamp-Glissando postulate is "uninterpretable" (p.258), "too vague for serious consideration" (p.617 fn.), and "so transparently fallacious as to boggle the mind" (p. 1164 et passim). For a parallel development in syntax, see Force(1968).

[16] In her less lucid moments (see the previous section, note 7), the informant sometimes spoke entirely in the Acc.Pl. for several hours at a sitting. The resultant effect was odd, but not unpleasing, rather like the taste of buckwheat groats pickled in slivovitz. For the symbolism involved and its significance for poetic theory, see Sapper (1921).

[17] One unusual facet of U that we have not previously remarked upon is the paucity of accidental gaps in the lexicon.

[18] One consequence of this move is that the logical flaw in the arguments of Hella (1961) and Hella (1962) (which purport to demonstrate that the assumption of a level of biunique phonemic representation situated between morphophonemic representation and phonetic representation results in the impossibility of capturing significant linguistic generalizations) is clearly exposed; the phonemic representations arrived at above are obviously biunique, yet no generalization capturable in Hella's (or even Chumsky's) so-called "non-taxonomic" model is not capturable in the sober, taxonomic model assumed above. But this point has been made so often in the literature that it would be otiose to repeat it here.

[19] By the Rare Book Room of the University of Illinois Library, Urbana, to which this writer takes his pleasure of expressing his gratitude.

[20] First suggested in private communications between Moras Hella and Toomis Beaver.

[21] Our discussion of this problem has been considerably illuminated by suggestions made by the great Hispanic polyhistor Juan Roberto de la Rosa.

[22] It is odd that rules of this type have not been discussed in the literature. They are formally about as simple as, or simpler than, such common rules as regressive voicing assimilation in stop clusters. It may be worth noticing that Urbanan has no voicing assimilation rule of any kind, even within morphemes (cf. IV-6 and VI-1). Urbanan also lacks the rather common rule of assimilation of nasals to the position of a following stop, even within morphemes (cf. IV-3). On both counts Urbanan is a much simpler language that either English or Russian, for example.

[23] At several points in the field work I suspected the existence of a Champaignese dialect, in which Rule (D) was restricted to high vowels only. However, our knowledge of the external history of the language is such that we must conclude that if there was such a dialect, it developed from the dialect reported herein. But Rule (D) in this dialect would be a restriction of the Urbanan Rule (D). According to Clippership's still unpublished but much discussed dictum that if a rule changes throughout time it changes by becoming more general, such a restriction is an impossible historical change. We much therefore conclude that Champaignese never existed.

REFERENCES

Bluebird, Jozef. (1953a) Obscene words for non-obscene body parts in Super-Saharan Africa. *IJAL*.

Bluebird, Jozef. (1953b) A branching index for roots. *Quantum Mechanics Monthly*.

Bluebird, Jozef. (1953c) On the wider linguistic affinities of Penutian. *Slippery Rock Publications in Anthropology*, No. 7.

Chumsky, Numb. (1957) *Structural Syntages*. Reading, Pa.

Chumsky, Numb and Moras Hella. *The Sound Pattern of Pig Latin*. Paestum.

Craft, Ebbing. (1966) *Spéculations sur les rapports linguistiques de la langue Urbane*. Epinal.

Force, Brutus. (1968) Quantifiers as quantifiers. Unpublished ms.

Glissando, Hermann. (1965) Second thoughts about phonemes. *Language*.

Hausa, Merry. (1951) *Obscene Terms for Non-Obscene Body Parts in Amerindian*. Occasional Publications of the Theosophical Society. Uxbridge, Mass.

Hella, Moras. (1961) Phrenology in generative glamor. *World* . Mossadegh Celebratory Volume.

Hella, Moras. (1962) A pocket-sized anti-phoneme proof. In *This Year in Science*. (ed. Yarmulka). Bantam Books and Grove Press.

Hen, Amalie. (1949) Queen Nokomis' love letters: the Urbano-Tektite hypothesis vindicated. *Classical Daily News* (June 14).

von Humbert Humbert, Humbert. (1802) *Über die Verschiedenheit des übermenschlichen Sprachbaues*. Bombay and Tunis.

Lamp, Surly. (1964) *An Introduction to Gratificational Stammer*. Biloxi, Miss.

Latsop, Laup. (1967) *Phonology of the Theory of Aspects*. Wildwood, N.J.

Pie, Mulberry. (1948) *The Wonder of Words and the Lasciviousness of Language*. Bayonne, N.J.

Pocketa-Queep, Charles ta. (1958) *An Introduction to Scientific Linguistics*. Burbank, Calif.

Pocketa-Queep, Charles ta. (1966) Review of *Diffraction and Dispersion* by Sir Lawrence Bragg,

Sapper, Edwin. (1921) The concept of phonesthetic Kasuslehre as tested by by Learned Broomfield. *Etc*.

NOTES ON CRAFT'S 'ON NOTATIONAL CONVENTIONS': CURRENT TRENDS IN URBANAN STUDIES

A. D. HOKE

Carmelite Mission of our Lady of the Starlings

The recent stimulating article by Craft[1] led me to reexamine some field notes which I collected during the Labor Day weekend of 1967, and has shed a new and quite unexpected light on the results of that work. The purpose of this paper is to report on the new and quite unexpected light shed on that work by the recent stimulating article by Craft.[2]

The informant was a 94-year-old woman whom I took to be of the ancient Natick-Cohasset stock on the basis of the characteristically narrow (2.91 cm.) interocular diameter, broad (6.17 cm.) patella, and argumentative temperament. She was unable or unwilling to divulge her name, which she claimed was unpronounceable[3] in her language. At the time I met her, she was engaged in diving from the pier of the Scripps Institute of Oceanography in search of Ipswich clams (with remarkably indifferent success, I might add). She claimed to be a lifelong resident of the area, saying that otherwise she would not be eligible to draw her weekly unemployment compensation, and attributed the fact that her neighbors pretended not to recognize her to churlish resentment at her recent elopement with the local B.I.A. agent. I was unable to ascertain the name of her tribe, since she insisted on referring to it as *zuikĩ* 'human being' (a clear indication of the ethnocentric, not to say chauvinistic, nay, xenophobic thought patterns of this primitive creature). Notwithstanding these difficulties, I was able to gain a fairly clear picture of the morphology and syntax of her native language, some of the more unusual features of which will be described here.

The phonology of her language, insofar as I was able to work it out,[4] was identical to that reported by Craft for Urbanan, with the exception that I did not detect phonemic pitch distinctions in the vowels.[5] This in itself is strongly indicative of a relationship. It is of further interest to note that my informant's language (henceforth L) contained all of the vocabulary items mentioned by Craft, with identical glosses. Surely many genetic relationships have been postulated on the basis of evidence no stronger than this. There are aspects of L not reported in Urbanan, however. Important among these is a highly productive morphological process whereby the C and C of CVC morphemes are interchanged. Thus working from the set of forms offered by Craft as illustrative of consonant distinctions in word-final position, we see the alternations *kap* 'fuzz' ~ *pak* 'pimple', *kat* 'chaise longue' ~ *tak* 'conversation, *kak* 'penis (of one's own)' ~ *kak* 'penis (of one's own), *kav* 'inscription' ~ *vak* 'grammatical category of direct address', *kaz* 'excuse' ~ *zak* 'cloth footcovering', *kaγ* 'wheel' ~ *γak* 'clearing of the throat', *kam* 'quiet' ~ *mak* 'turtle soup', *kan* 'resort' ~ *nak* 'malfunction in an internal combustion engine', *kaŋ* 'ape' ~ *ŋak* 'Vietnamese', *kal* 'telephone message' *lak* 'segment (as of a canal)'. The semantic force of this alternation scarcely needs elucidation. Some points deserve mention, however. Note first of all that the alternation does not take place in just those cases where it would result in the placement of *f s x b d g* in the forbidden initial position: thus *kab* 'rind' but **bak*, *kaf* 'husky voice' but **fak*,[7] etc. This is a striking example of the operation of put-out conditions of the sort proposed by Nacre (1968). Secondly, observe that this alternation is a paradigm instance of the sort of Item-and-Arrangement morphophonemics outlined by Pockeeta-Queep (1964) and most naturally provided for within the notational conventions of Lamp (1966), thus militating against the process morphophonemics of Chumsky and Hella (1968). Furthermore, since only one "rule"[8] is involved, it is impossible, not just unnecessary, to impose ordering, again supporting Lamp.

The syntax of L boasts a phenomenon which is, so far as I know, unique among the languages of the world. Whenever a native speaker of L is asked to repeat himself, in the repetition he restores all of the transformationally deleted and rearranged elements to their original position. The result, of course, is that the repetition consists of the terminal string of the pre-transformational[9] structure of the sentence being repeated. The actual existence of this phenomenon, known in the literature as undeletable reconstruction, confirms a conjecture by Mathe-Hughes (1963). I first became aware of its existence in L when I asked my informant to repeat the sentence I had transcribed as *vloid uxlẽpa ɣmult* 'Floyd broke the poi-jar'. The repetition was *nmoklẽzan pzili tfaxud tfaxud tfaxud vloid zsuŋilf tfaxud vloid lixlevm tfaxud tfaxud pixnepa mukzmlit tfaxud pixnepa ɣmulg i lusglã aoifoe azlfilp mnoklẽzan* 'I declare it it it Floyd do it Floyd cause it it poi-jar be it poi-jar break *i*[10] happen have to you'. Needless to say, this fascinating phenomenon could be extremely time-consuming. One entire informant session was taken up when I inadvertently asked for a repetition of *ku pibũ pluvn zuvõna tlitlitlit* '7,847 prime ministers kissed their respective mothers'.

At the end of the three-day weekend, when I had completed my field notes, I bade farewell to my nameless informant, little dreaming that at some distant point in aboriginal antiquity, her forebears must have been intimate with the inhabitants of the ancient city of gold, *kxoⁿin* 'Peoria' (Acc.Pl.).

NOTES

[1] Craft (1968).

[2] Ibid.

[3] Her exact phrase was "an impossible [sic] form".

[4] I have always been a bit weak in phonology.

[5] I did notice, however, a marked peculiarity in her intonational patterns, a sort of "sing-song" quality as compared with, say, English. See note 4.

[6] This form is also found in the untranslatable expletive *zak itumi*.

[7] Based on the general onamatopoetic patterning of the language, one might

have predicted this as a plausible form for 'copulation'. That morph, however, turns out to be e (Acc.Pl.) in L just as in Urbanan.

[8] The quotation marks are used to signal the author's awareness that this is, after all, merely a convenient fictional construct. See Homeowner (1963).

[9] One hesitates to say "deep", in view of Coughlake and Force (1967).

[10] i is a metalinguistic circumlocution meaning "designated representative of the class of inchoative verbs".

REFERENCES

Chumsky, Numb and Moras Hella. (1968) *The Sound Pattern of Pig Latin*. Paestum.

Coughlake, Gorge, and Brutus Force. (1967) Sont-ils nécessaires les structures profondes? Unpublished memo, Tierra del Fuego.

Craft, Ebbing. (1968) On notational conventions: new evidence from the field. Papeete. Reprinted in this volume.

Homeowner, Freud. (1963) On prim linguists. *Die Kunst der Sprache*.

Lamp, Surly. (1966) Epilegomena to any future prolegomena. In Sebeok (ed.), *Festschrift for Pāṇini*. Addis Ababa.

Mathe-Hughes, Hughes. (1963) Symmetrical asymmetry and the all-or-none. *Hasidic Quarterly*.

Nacre, Goliath. (1968) *Put-out Conditions in English and Other Exotic Tongues*. Unpublished D.H.L. dissertation, University of the Seven Seas.

Pockeeta-Queep, Charles ta. (1964) *Entropy Reexamined in the Light of Polyunique Strata*. Rangoon and Osawatomie, Kansas.

UP AGAINST THE WALL, FASCIST PIG CRITICS!

EBBING CRAFT
Old School for Social Research[0]

In a much-misunderstood paper (Craft 1968) published two years ago in an unfortunately rather obscure series, I argued for the essential correctness of a view of grammatical theory due to the young American polymath Numb Chumsky. According to this view, which I hereby christen the Erector Set (British Meccano) Proposal, grammatical theory provides a collection of constructional units (called notational conventions) together with a box of tools (called formal universals) for combining these units so as to form a Ferris wheel (called a grammatical description). The goal of grammatical theory is to find the right set of units and the right box of tools -- namely, the ones that can be used to build any possible Ferris wheel, and no non-Ferris wheels. The objectives of my earlier essay were (a) to affirm this goal in a general way, and (b) to demonstrate the correctness of some specific nuts-and-bolts proposals in the literature, by adducing phonological processes in a language, Urbanan, which can be described by previously unattested combinations of notational conventions permitted in standard theories.

These modest objectives have been viciously, and quite wrong-headedly, attacked in print on a number of occasions. Allow me to dispose by my assailants, beginning with the most nit-picking of them.

In my hastily composed note, or squid, in the new journal *Linguistic Liberty*, the upstart syntactician In Rē Junkitall (1970) rejects my masterpiece because it draws upon phenomena in a language not understanded of the people (i.e., one significantly distinct from English), and most especially because my discussion was based upon work with the last speaker of the language (who, most regrettably, had died by the time of publication). Even for a squid, this is an arm-waving argument. It flies in the face of the finest traditions of anthropological linguistics and is undoubtedly racist (probably sexist[1] to boot, for my late informant was a woman). I mention Junkitall's attack only because similar criticisms have been advanced by our mentor Chumsky; I do not mean to suggest that there might be any validity in such narrow-minded parochialism.

More serious, but nevertheless invalid, attacks have been mounted by a handful of scholars -- among them Davide Francobollo and Lemon Block. Francobollo, in a justly celebrated series of unwritten masterworks (Francobollo, to be written a, to be written b, to be written c), opposes the Erector Set Proposal (hereafter ESP) on philosophical grounds, none of them sufficiently coherent to allow of an unemotional response on my part. I gather, though, that like Block, he feels that the ESP does not permit satisfactorily substantive claims about language and that it does not suggest real explanations, whatever they might be. He also appears to have some irrational doubts about the simplicity metric. To all this I say: pooh. There is a child in each of us that wants strong substantive claims; the ESP has the virtue of not pampering that child. As for explanation,

what does Francobollo want? It has taken us fifty long years to realize
fully that linguistics must be absolutely autonomous (even the great Franco-
German pre-phonemicist Schuman Pool[2] perceived this transparent truth only
dimly); we should not be led back into the Dark Ages by a neo-Mediaeval
philosopher masquerading as a phonologist. Finally, the simplicity metric
is so obviously good and beautiful that it must be true.

Francobollo does cite some interesting examples, both his own and
some from Sickly (1969), but of course these phenomena can be described
quite handily within classic ESP.

Block (1970a; cf. Block 1970b and 1970c) cavils at me in much the
same fashion. Both he and Francobollo subscribe to the preposterous and
empirically untestable view that linguistic theory is a finite list of
rules, which are (is?), moreover, innate. To state this proposal is to
refute it. Nonetheless, Block pushes on and formulates what he calls the
Universal Curse, the properties of which he proposes to explain on the
basis of proferred pseudo-generalizations about universal syntax and
semantics. For example, he intends to explain the fact [sic] that curses
are unidirectional (speaker to addressee, never the reverse) on the grounds
that de la Rosa's Convex Subject Constraint (de la Rosa 1967) would prohibit the flow of an impulse into an ovoid ordered or (a fat speaker, for
instance). Grok, I say. How can one explain the properties of an artefact?
And have the gall to advance in support a tissue of falsities? [3]

The transcendent truth of my position has been buttressed time and
again, most recently by the splendid work being accomplished in progressive
(as opposed to regressive, although of course no directionality is implied)
semantics. I refer here not so much to the writings of McQuarrelly, whose
thought is not always sound dogmatically, but rather to the output of
Coughlake, that prolific exponent of generative power (see, inter alia,
Coughlake to appear a, to appear b, to appear N_0). Coughlake's irrefutable,
nay absolutely crushing, indications of the necessity for wholly novel
forms of grammatical apparatus -- approximately one total revolution in
theory each week, beginning with the Ann Arbor Film Festival winter,
Durational Constraints -- quite boggle the mind. Nothing could prove
the correctness of the ESP more convincingly than these repeated demons-
trations that the required pulleys must be larger and stronger than we
were inclined to believe.

NOTES

[0] Formerly of the Hamtramck School for Girls. I am especially indebted
to A. D. Hoke, whose response (1968) to my earlier article sustained
my sometimes lonely battle against an unsympathetic and antediluvian
Establishment; Professor Hoke's martyrdom (his attack of terminal aphasia
was obviously brought on by the scurrilous screed *Hoke Has Poked Us* (two
vols.) directed against him by that Establishment arch-villain Laup Latsop)
should serve as a reminder to us all that those in power will stop at
nothing to still the voice of freedom, truth, peace, and love. I am also
indebted to Sole Support, editor of the "pop" journal of Indo-Iranian
metrics *Philology Shmilology*, for his unflagging criticism, and to my
graduate research assistant, Churls Quibblesworth, for changing my type-

writer ribbon and keeping the flagons full. The above are, of course, responsible for some of the errors in the present paper. In particular, Support's misunderstanding of Francobollo's work was directly reflected in my discussion of it, and upon Quibblesworth falls the responsibility for the incorrect citations of the second and sixth items in the bibliography. On the other hand, I am personally culpable for the total neglect of Wierdisch's work, which neglect completely vitiates my arguments. By the time this material was written up, no one was able to recall which of us had forgotten to cite the parallel (if not identical) approach in Marquart 1954.

[1] See the recent provocative report by Clean-a-Beluga and Partly.

[2] Novel Yarmulka relates an amusing anecdote involving Pool and his wily antagonist Fer de l'Ans de Saucière: At the 1899 meeting of Die Lumpengesellschaft für Wörter und Sachen in neutral Alsace, l'Ans de Saucière rose to toast Pool with the words, "a notre Pool". Pool took the remark to refer to Lady Wobbly, the only Lady present, and communicated his intentions toward her in rather too direct a fashion. This incident is not mentioned even in l'Ans de Saucière's scandalous *Mémoire*. I can't imagine why I have mentioned it.

[3] As Pocketa-Queep has been kind enough to impress upon me, there is only one real generalization known about language: At one time, one person was known to communicate by means of a vocal noise with another person. By an ingenious use of the K-Saunaglyph, Ladderfogle (1970) has identified the noise as [ŋ']. Attempts at dating the event with standard glottochronological methods have thus far failed, due to the sloppiness of the procedures (see Palestinensis 1956). The observer is popularly supposed to have been Dolly Pentreath, but this is a lie. There are many lacunae to be filled here. To the ramparts, Linguist!

REFERENCES

Block, Lemon. (1970a) Curses about curses. *Bucca* 1:270-3 et passim.

Block, Lemon. (1970b) Unverhandelbare Forderungen über unverhandelbare Forderungen. *Zeitschr. f. Akad. Philos. u. Allgem. Wissensch.* MMCCLXVIII:cxx-cxlvi.

Block, Lemon. (1970c) Un petit bouquet d'avertissement sur les avertissements. *Luggages* 1:1-103.

Clean-a-Beluga, Bärchen and B. Haul Partly. (1973) *Manifeste contre sexisme: Sales cochons de linguistes masculins*. Port Huron.

Coughlake, Gorge. (To appear a) Natural logic and unnatural linguistics.

Coughlake, Gorge. (To appear b) On the factual inadequacy of all theoretical positions in linguistics, this one included.

Coughlake, Gorge. (To appear $\aleph_0$) The straight truth about quantifiers, and other heavy facts about high predicates.

Craft, Ebbing. (1968) On notational conventions: new evidence from the field. *Papeete Newsletter for Esthetics and Dying Languages* 13:14-20a.

Hoke, A.D. (1968) Notes on Craft's 'On notational conventions': current trends in Urbanan studies. *Bull. Kwak. Studs.* 204:3923-7.

Francobollo, Davide. (To be written a) On the theory of nurtural phonology.

Francobollo, Davide. (To be written b) Recent trends in nurtural phonology.

Francobollo, Davide. (To be written c) Aspects of the dreary in phonology.

Junkitall, In Rë. (1970) Why Craft lacks it, and other problems in his frame of reference: on the consequences of failing to groove with Professor Chumsky. *Linguistic Liberty* 1:26.

Ladderfogle, Petty. (1970) Phonetics to the rescue, a case study. *J.L.A. P.D.Res.Dev.* 16:49-6 [played in reverse].

Marquart, Don. (1954) *What the hill, Archie!* San Juan.

Robertus Palenstinensis [né Urbanensis]. (1956) Sloppiness as an exact concept in glottochronology, and other regrets. *Phrase* 20:11-43±2.

Rosa, Juan Roberto de la. (1967) *Restraint in variable syntax.* Unfinished Ph.D. thesis, Center for Appliquéed and Otherwise Embellished Linguistics.

Sickly, Old. (1969) Note on a phonological bureaucracy in the Middle West. *Historical Linguistics from the Eclipsing Stance of Transformational Grammar,* ed. R(eceived) P(ronunciation) Stickwell. Indian University Press: Window Rock and Hyderabad.

ON CONCRETE SYNTAX*

ČABNOMME

Seven[1] arguments are presented here to show that the most abstract[2] representations of a sentence are of a complexity hitherto undreamt of by anybody. The special topic of our investigation is the subset of English sentences having to do with cement, but the conclusions are readily generalizable. We shall see that there are certain regularities in subordinate sentences of this syntacto-semantic class and then argue that to characterize nonembedded sentences of the same sort without Missing Generalizations it is necessary to posit abstract (or better concrete, see note 2) embedding sentences that disappear without an overt trace.

A.   Embedded cement sentences (ECS for short) frequently mention *sand* and this substantive frequently occurs in the embedding context. Thus we have

(1) "Better add more sand," said Harold as he handed Seymour a bucket of sand.

(2) I thought that the stuff should have more sand so I looked slowly at Pilar and told her that it should have more sand and then I saw that she had heard me say that it should have more sand and that she was adding more sand because you have to know that cement takes sand and if something is going to be truly good then it has to have what it takes.

Notice that sentences with some other word in place of *sand* are odd.

(3) ?*"Better add more sand," said Harold as he handed Seymour a bucket of Wheaties.

(4) ?*"Better add more Wheaties," said Harold as he handed Seymour a bucket of sand.

(5) ?*The stuff needed more sand, so Sally added more gravel.

Notice that in each case of the first type we find an occurrence of the word *sand* in the embedding context and the same word *sand* -- and not some arbitrary word like *salmon* or *postprandium* -- in the embedded sentence. Moreover, when we substitute some other word, as in (3) - (5), the result is an odd sentence. This cooccurrence must be accounted for somehow. Since the argument is rather complex, let us summarize this finding as

FACT I.   There is a restriction on occurrences of the word *sand* in ECS and the ECS-embedding context.

Now let us turn to non-embedded cement sentences (NCS). Here we notice the inexplicable fact that exactly the same distribution of oddity occurs. Thus in the real world context of people mixing cement, eating breakfast, etc., we would make the following judgments:

(6) Better add more sand.

(7) It should have more sand.

(8) She's adding more sand.

(9) ?*Better add more sand. (said at breakfast)

(10) ?*Better add more Wheaties. (said while mixing cement)

Let us list this as

FACT II. NCS mention *sand* (and not Wheaties, etc.).

Summarizing, then, we have

FACT I. There is a restriction on occurrences of the word *sand* in ECS and the ECS-embedding context.

FACT II. NCS mention *sand* (and not Wheaties, etc.).

Now there are three logical possibilities with respect to FACTS I and II. We can

(a) ignore them;
(b) give a separate explanation for FACT I and FACT II;
(c) give a uniform explanation for FACTS I and II.

Clearly, any serious linguist will opt for (c). But then it is impossible to escape the conclusion that the underlying representations of NCS are actually ECS, and that the underlying representations include at least this much structure:

(11) ...SAND...S

where SAND is an abstract element almost, but not quite, like the element *sand*. SAND is like *sand* in that it occurs in the deepest representation of CS,[3] but unlike it in that it occurs only in the context of NCS. Thus we do not have

(12) *This rope is made of SAND.

(13) *This rope is made of.

Now it is straightforward to satisfy requirement (c) and give a uniform explanation for the *sand*-FACTS I and II. Notice that the fact that I do not know what specific rules or constraints are necessary to account for the regularities does not invalidate the argument. This is because the fact that I do not know the rules is a fact about me and not about English and hence could not conceivably play a role in any deduction about linguistic facts.

Arguments B, C, D, E, and F, can be constructed quite easily by the reader by substituting for *sand*: *cement, water, gravel, shovel,* and *bucket* (with obvious adjustments in the examples).

We have now established that there must be a structure of roughly the following sort associated at the deepest levels with every NCS:

(14)   ...SAND...CEMENT...WATER...GRAVEL...SHOVEL...BUCKET...S

We have so far treated the abstract elements as unanalyzed entities, but they obviously have a great deal to do with each other and with, respectively, the real elements *sand, cement, water, gravel, shovel, bucket.*[4] We may therefore assume that they are actually collections of feature specifications, in particular that each has the specification [+ABSTRACT] which marks them as undergoing a deletion rule. This fact leads us to the most powerful argument for our analysis.[5]

G.   If we did not posit the abstract elements above, it would be impossible to state the following highly general principle:

(37')   For any element A_i $(i > 1)$ such that A_i occurs in P-markers P_k $(k > 1)$ and is marked [+Abstract] there must be a rule R such that if A_i is the jth term $(i \leq j \leq n,$ where n is the number of terms in the structure index of R) in the proper analysis of P_k w.r.t. R, then the structural change of R must include the elementary transformation $t = (j,e)$ where e denotes the null string.

In nontechnical language Principle (37') states that for any element that occurs in a given phrase-marker and is marked as an abstract element there must be a rule such that if that element is in a certain position in that phrase-marker according to the analysis of that phrase-marker by the structural analysis of the transformation in question then the set of elementary transformations associated with that transformation must include one which has the effect of deleting -- i.e., replacing by null -- the element that occurs in that position of that phrase-marker according to its analysis by the structural analysis of that transformation (according to that grammar, of course).

Notice that we could not even state Principle (37') without the analysis that we have suggested for NCS!

If should be borne in mind that Argument G, repeated here for convenience:

G.   If we did not posit the abstract elements above [i.e., those mentioned in Arguments A - F], it would be impossible to state the following highly general principle [Principle (37')].

goes far beyond the usual arguments for particular analyses since, in effect, it states that there is a general, probably universal principle which leads us to select this analysis over others that could be proposed. Moreover, we can predict that other elements of this same sort will be found and thus 'reinforce' our 'concrete' analysis with a wide range of disparate facts.[6]

The only possible alternative treatment that I can imagine is the following. N. Chomsky, following a number of his students, has proposed an extension to the theory of linguistics that would allow us to add an 'interpretive' rule at any point in a grammar to do anything we wish. Since there are no published examples of such rules, I am free to add straw to my cement (so to speak) and invent a rule. Such a rule might be

(15)   Sentences about cement-mixing are about cement-mixing.

There are two possibilities to consider at this point. Semantic representations are P-markers or they are some new and different kind of object. Suppose they are P-markers. Then all the arguments given above go through and we must still posit an abstract structure underlying NCS. Suppose they are some different kind of object. Then we must have two totally different sets of principles or rules, one for the ECS (which are clearly P-markers) and one for the semantic representations of the NCS. I.e., we cannot meet requirement (c), repeated here for convenience:

(c) give uniform explanations for FACTS I and II, repeated here for convenience:

FACT I. There is a restriction on occurrences of the word *sand* in ECS and ECS-embedding contexts.

FACT II. NCS mention *sand* (and not Wheaties, etc.).

(Notice that we can cite Facts I', II', I", II", etc. for the elements mentioned in Arguments B - F as well). Thus, however we interpret (15) we find ourselves driven back to the conclusions reached above.

But recall Argument G. Argument G makes no reference to anything at all except the existence of a universal principle and the particular abstract elements we have set up. Therefore, it is quite independent of our hypotheses about semantics, interpretive, generative, or astrological. Thus, no matter what possible wrinkle or modification one might add to linguistic theory, our conclusions must stand.

I pointed out above the explanatory power of Principle (37') (notice that Rule (15) has no such predictive power at all). We would expect to find many situations in which we are led to set up abstract elements to explain regularities in all sorts of sentences. This prediction is borne out. So far we have investigated sentences about such diverse subjects as nuclear engineering, cooking, copulation, and lycanthropy. In each case we have been able to argue convincingly for the existence of such abstract elements as BOMB, THYME, DIAPHRAGM, FANG. Thus it seems as if the general direction of our research is correct. Most recently we have begun to do research on sentences about sentences, that is, linguistic discourse itself. Since such discourse forms a superset for any discourse whatsoever it should be possible to provide a general proof for the existence of a general proof for the existence of a general proof for the ...

NOTES

* The research reported on here was supported in part by NSF Grant GS
  2468. This is a preliminary report on ongoing research so that for
anyone to quote it is definitely unfair.

[1] Some readers may have different judgments from mine about these arguments. I should like to emphasize that I am discussing here one dialect, in which all of the following arguments are considered valid. Since
at least one such dialect exists, linguistic theory must accept my conclusions.

[2] Actually 'concrete' would for reasons to be discussed directly be a
  much more appropriate designation for the theory of deeper representa-
tation that is defended here.

[3] That is, cement sentences. I accept the arguments of Postal that NCS
  and ECS are indeed both CS; see his forthcoming paper 'Anaphorous Reefs.'

[4] This analysis only touches the surface of the complexities of CS.
  Notice, for example, that we have no explanation as yet for the fact
that precisely this collection of feature specifications occurs in the
deep representation of CS, and not, say, the above together with an
abstract element SALT. This complexity is hardly surprising in view of
the complexity of the English Stress Rule. Note further the difficulties
inherent in any attempt to account for such complex deep representations
according to any naive theories of 'induction,' 'habit,' or the like. See
Plato's *Meno* for an eloquent early statement of our position on this
question.

[5] I am indebted to my student S. Quirt for loaning me Argument G from
  his forthcoming thesis.

[6] In fact, a number of linguists have proposed analyses using such abstract
  elements. See also the last paragraph of this paper for a preliminary
report on further research which tends not to disconfirm our present hypotheses.

WHERE DO PROPER NAMES COME FROM?
(IN CASE THERE ARE ANY)[*]

I. M. CRATYLUS
Center for Nonverbal Communication
Upstate New York

There is an alarming conspiracy growing in this country -- not a conspiracy of grammatical rules, but one of linguists and philosophers -- and it must be checked before it gets out of hand. The fearful trend I am concerned about is the creeping (and creepy) view that all linguistic units are derived from verbs in the deep structure. I wish to show that proponents of the All-the-World's-a-Verb view are mistaken.

Trends in this direction began in harmless and plausible enough ways. For example, agentive nominals were derived from underlying verbs or verb phrases. Lees (1960:152), for example, proposed the following derivation:

(1) John teaches science. ———>
     John is a teacher of science. ———>
     ... teacher of science ... ———>
     ... science teacher ...

Assuming that transformations do not affect meaning and that everything semantically relevant is either in the base or the lexicon, the above derivation provides a passable semantic interpretation only if all the subtleties and nuances are ignored. For instance, John may be a science teacher only in that he lists 'science teacher' on his income tax form and is employed to teach science. However, it may be the case that when he meets with his classes, instead of teaching science he reads them pornolinguistic essays and brainwashes them into believing that Columbus discovered America in 1592. Yet one cannot automatically add the marker (Occupation) to agentive nominalizations, since in

(2) John fucks his mother. ———>
     John is a motherfucker.

no occupation is (necessarily) involved.

The next step in attempting to derive everything from verbs occurred when linguists argued that adjectives are really a kind of verb. From a semantic and logical point of view there is some plausibility in this hypothesis since both can serve as predicates. (Adjectives need the copula in addition, of course.) As Lyons (1968:325) points out, in some languages a distinction between verbs and adjectives cannot be made at all on morphological or distributional grounds. Lakoff (1966) argues that in terms of meaning, selection restrictions, stativity, nominalizations, object deletion, and FLIP, verbs and adjectives share so many things in common that their differences are comparatively trivial.

As Bach (1968:117) has pointed out, the stative-nonstative distinction is shared by predicate nouns as well as verbs and adjectives. One test of stativity is co-occurrence with the progressive aspect. Stative verbs, adjectives, and nouns do not occur in progressive constructions, while nonstatives do so freely. Compare the following:

(3) a. Harvey was screwing three Bennington girls simultaneously at Martha's orgy. [nonstative verb]

b. *I`am understanding that the drugstore has a sale on lemon-flavored Orthocream this week. [stative verb]

c. The students are being careful to not get VD at Martha's orgy. [nonstative adjective]

d. *Harvey was being impotent at Martha's orgy. [stative adjective]

e. George is being a fool by studying philosophy when he could blow his mind faster by taking LSD. [nonstative predicate noun]

f. *George is being a mammal.[1] [stative predicate noun]

A second argument by Lakoff to show that adjectives are verbs is that both verbs and adjectives share certain contextual restrictions (animate subject plus animate verb or adjective; physical object subject plus a certain subclass of verbs and adjectives; etc.). However, these restrictions apply to agreement between subjects and predicate nominals, too.

(4) a. John is a lecher.
b. *John is an orgasm.

(5) a. This rock is a mineral.
b. *This rock is an abstract verb.

Yet to treat *lecher*, *orgasm*, *mineral*, and *verb* as underlying verbs has none of the plausibility of Lees' derivation of *teacher*.

A third argument for collapsing adjectives and verbs into one class is that verbs and adjectives in relative clauses can be shifted to prenominal position:

(6) The man who was queer ⟶ the queer man.

But the same is true of nouns in relative clauses:

(7) The friend who is a boy ⟶ the boyfriend.

A proposal even more subversive than those above is proposed by Jonnie Geis and Michael Geis. They argue that prepositions are deep structure verbs.

The analysis that I am presupposing for sentences containing locative and temporal phrases is that prepositions are transitive,

subject-embedding verbs in deep structure and that prepositional
phrases are deep structure verb phrases. (J. Geis, 1970:227)

M. Geis (1970:248) assumes a similar point of view but still wonders why
verbs and prepositions seem to be so different, if in fact they both
belong to the same underlying category.

The principal motivation for treating prepositions as verbs seems
to be that prepositions, like transitive verbs, are subject to co-occurrence
restrictions with the following nouns:

    (8) a. The dean laid the students at the flagpole.

        b. *The dean laid the students at the first page of the
           Kama Sutra.

        c. All Kant scholars have memorized the *Kama Sutra*.

        d. *All Kant scholars have memorized the flagpole.

However, other word classes are also restricted by following nouns
-- determiners, for example:

    (9) a. this asshole   *this assholes
        b. *a vice-presidents   some vice-president

By the criterion suggested above, we should treat determiners as deep
structure verbs. (Of course, since Lakoff (1970) and Carden (1967) have
argued that quantifiers are deep structure predicates, it is not all that
much of an existential leap to hold the view that all determiners are
deep structure verbs. This shows how subtlely the conspirators have
operated to destroy the critical abilities of American linguistics students.)

If we look at the function of prepositions in English by comparing
English noun phrases with other languages, especially highly synthetic
ones (Latin, Classical Greek, Sanskrit, Estonian, Hungarian, Turkish,
Finnish, Lithuanian, etc.) it is clear that prepositions function like
case endings. If anyone proposes that the Finnish illative is really a
deep structure verb, that proves that the integrity of grammatical foundations as well as the moral fibre of grammarians has already been under-
mined, and the enemy can take over at any time.

Finally I wish to turn to the topic of greatest danger, that of
names. One of the radical conspirators, Quine, suggested that it might
be possible to eliminate proper names by treating them as predicates or
even verbs. Quine's purpose, which need not concern us here, is basically
an attempt at ontological population control, to keep the universe from
being peopled with Santa Claus, Pegasus, and the Seven Dwarfs.

In order thus to subsume a one-word name or alleged name
such as 'Pegasus' under Russell's theory of description, we
must, of course, be able first to translate the word into a
description. But this is no real restriction. If the notion
of Pegasus had been so obscure or so basic a one that no pat
translation into a descriptive phrase had offered itself along

familiar lines, we could still have availed ourselves of the
following artificial and trivial-seeming device: we could have
appealed to the *ex hypothesi* unanalyzable, irreducible attribute
of *being Pegasus*, adopting, for its expression, the verb 'is
Pegasus', or 'pegasizes'. The noun 'Pegasus' itself could then
be treated as derivative and identified after all with a description, 'the thing that is Pegasus', 'the thing that pegasizes'.
(Quine, 1953:7-8)

It seems simple to find a counterexample to Quine's argument that
all names can be treated as predicates. Let us imagine that an outstanding
citizen from Los Angeles named John Bullshit is a very truthful person
and consider the sentence

(10)   Bullshit doesn't bullshit.

This sentence is clearly synthetic and might be true. According to Quine,
that sentence would translate into another sentence where the name Bullshit becomes the predicate bullshit, and the sentence reduces to

(11) $(\exists x)$ (x bullshits and x does not bullshit)

I.e., there exists an x such that x bullshits and x does
not bullshit, which is certainly contradictory.

Quine might reply that the counterexample is trivial because *x
bullshits* is ambiguous between the two uses of the predicate. The first
reply to Quine is that it does not seem to be the case that *x bullshits*
is in fact ambiguous, and speakers would understand the sentence only
as a predication about x. But more importantly, if the phrase is ambiguous,
the only way to disambiguate it is to point out that one sense predicates
something about x, namely that he bullshits, and the other sense is a
special way of identifying x -- by saying he is Bullshit. Even though
Quine wants to eliminate names, he must eventually bring them in to disambiguate certain predicates like *x bullshits*, which only became ambiguous
through Quine's semantic shenanigans.[2]

Well, where does that leave us with respect to the Everything-is-
a-Verb Conspiracy? It is true that other parts of speech share certain
features with verbs, and pointing out such similarities is an interesting
and valuable contribution. But the facts certainly do not warrant the
conclusion that therefore nouns and adjectives and prepositions and proper
names and whatever else must be verbs. We must distinguish between formal
word classes like verbs and nouns and functional notions such as predication and modification. It is true that nouns, adjectives, and verbs
may all occur in predications and all may be used as modifiers. But to
conclude that because nouns, adjectives, prepositions, etc. share certain
features with verbs they must be considered deep structure verbs is exactly
the tactic used by subversive conspirators. It is the guilt by association
technique which spreads fear and confusion. (In all probability, it is
supported by Maoists, in whose language adjectives and verbs can reasonably
be collapsed.) It is the same logic used by a certain vice-president (who
shall remain unnamed) when he insinuates that all long-haired youth who
like rock music are anti-American, draft-dodging, enemy-comfort-giving,
brownshirt, bomb-throwing radicals.

The conspiracy is even more dangerous, however, for if everything is a verb, then verbs themselves lose their identity and are nothing special. And that would surely be tragic.

In view of this growing danger, I urge every linguist, philosopher, and citizen concerned with preserving our traditional grammatical values to contact his local professional organizations and demand that something be done immediately.

NOTES

* This research was supported in part by a grant by the Antiverbalization League, the Society for the Preservation of Deep Structure Prepositions, and the Senate Subcommittee on Un-Grammatical Activities.

[1] However, the acceptability of *George is being an animal at Martha's orgy* should be obvious to anyone familiar with the specified form of socialization.

[2] I am indebted to Professor Antiquine for this argument.

REFERENCES

Bach, Emmon. (1968) Nouns and noun phrases. *Universals in Linguistic Theory*, ed. Bach and Harms. New York: Holt, Rinehart & Winston. 90-122.

Carden, Guy. (1967) Quantifiers as higher verbs. Unpublished M.A. thesis, Harvard University.

Geis, Jonnie. (1970) Lexical insertion of locative and time prepositions. *Papers from the Sixth Regional Meeting, Chicago Linguistic Society*. Chicago: University of Chicago. 226-34.

Geis, Michael. (1970) Time prepositions as underlying verbs. *Papers from the Sixth Regional Meeting, Chicago Linguistic Society*. Chicago: University of Chicago: University of Chicago. 235-49.

Lakoff, George. (1965) *On the Nature of Syntactic Irregularity*. Mathematical Linguistics and Automatic Translation, Report No. NSF-16. Harvard University Computation Laboratory.

Lakoff, George. (1970) 'Repartee' or a reply to 'Negation, conjunction, and quantifiers'. *Foundations of Language* 6:389-422.

Lees, Robert B. (1960) *The Grammar of English Nominalizations* (=IJAL 26, No. 3, Part II).

Lyons, John. (1968) *Introduction to Theoretical Linguistics*. Cambridge: Cambridge University Press.

Quine, Willard Van Orman. (1953) *From a Logical Point of View*. Cambridge, Mass.: Harvard University Press.

ON THE NOTION "DERIVATIONAL CONSTRAINT OF GRAMMAR"
OR:
THE TURING MACHINE DOESN'T STOP HERE ANYMORE (IF IT EVER WILL)

ROBERT WALL
University of Texas at Austin

In this paper[1] I will presuppose a grammar of the customary generative syntax-to-semantics, variably constrained, input-and-output conditoned, serially lexiconned, but idiom-monitored, transformational-generative sort which has by now become reasonably familiar,[2] and which, despite repeated claims to the contrary,[3] represents nothing more than a return to the deeply insightful, albeit completely misguided, attempts of early Corsican scholars to establish a universal theory of language based on the rationalist, quasi-empiricist doctrines and the general social and intellectual disorder of the Twelfth and Thirteenth Centuries.[4] To quote Alacarte:

> Voilà le grand auto de mon oncle! C'est joli, ça,
> n'est-ce pas? C'est un Moustang extraordinaire. Ça
> marche très fortement, je te dis![5]

It was largely a departure from this tradition which led to the abandonment of interest in the quite serious program of determining universal constraints on constraints, and substituted in its place an over-emphasis on anti-empiricist, verificationist dogmatism under which American linguistics labored during the dark years of the early part of the Twentieth Century.[6] I emphasize this point because it is one of the important notions underlying the theory of transformational-generative grammar which, to my knowledge, has never been misunderstood by anyone.[7] It seems to me that all claims to the contrary are wholly without empirical support and that the burden of proof falls, as usual, on those who disagree.[8]

Recently, controversy has centered on the notoriously vexatious question of the directionality of derivations, and, hence, of derivational constraints, By 'derivational constraint' I refer to the entirely delusional notion coined by Coughlake *et seq.* to account for the previously unexplained fact that no one else in the entire world speaks his dialect.[9] In the earliest literature on the subject only the west-to-east direction was posited, because it was, quite simply, the only direction available at the time. With the attainment of recent results in recursive function theory, however, it has at last become possible to think coherently of an east-to-west orientation of the phrase-markers in a derivation, and with this advance has come, quite naturally, uncertainty as to which of those hypotheses, if either, is correct. I will refer to the east-to-west (EW) hypothesis as the Big End or Everywhere Adequate position and to its contrary as the Little End or Hopelessly Stupid position (HSP). There is no significance whatever attached to this purely terminological choice of epithets.[10] For lack of space I will not discuss alternatives other than these, although it should be noted that in the rudimentary state of our knowledge even so superficially implausible a suggestion as that of north-to-south cannot be definitely ruled out on a *priori* grounds.[11]

Put briefly, Coughlake, along with others who hold the HSP, maintains that the trees in a derivation such as

(1) $P_1, P_2, P_3, \ldots, P_n$

are oriented from left-to-right, whereas the Everywhere Adequate hypothesis holds that this is not necessarily not untrue, although elsewhere both parties have argued, convincingly it seems to me, that it doesn't really matter (or else both are wrong). At this level of generality it appears that there is little more that can be said about the question (although Beaver has argued recently that the level of generality should not be considered relevant in scientific discussion[12]). It is, of course, to be expected that one can increase the complexity of going from west-to-east with a corresponding decrease in the complexity of going from east-to-west (maintaining the position of the page constant, of course), and vice versa. There is nothing the least bit surprising in this result, which has been characteristic of every science from the time of Babylonian astronomy to contemporary metaphysics. East has always been to the right and west to the left. Apparent counterexamples, such as ancient Arabic maps in which south is at the top and thus with the corresponding positions of east and west reversed, have been shown on closer inspection to be of doubtful origin (*unbekannter Herausstellung*), and, far from refuting the EW hypothesis, actually support it. There is a great deal more to be said on this question, but I will not pursue the matter any further here.

We should note, first of all, that the question as to the direction of derivations is a wholly empirical one. Which is right and which is wrong (or left) is a matter of fact, not of definition.[13] Thus, it is reasonable to inquire whether there are empirical observations which can be brought to bear on this question. There are, in fact, as can be seen by comparing the sentences in (2) with those in (3):

(2) a. Bill criticized John's book, although he had not read
        (any of) it (at all) (*whatever).
    b. Bill knew John, although he had never met him.

(3) a. *Bill criticized his book, although John had not read it
        (found it in the street, returned it to the library).
    b. *Bill knew him, although John had never met Bill.

The ungrammaticality of the starred sequences in (3) is based on the interpretation in which *his* and *him* are co-referential with *John*.[14] I am not here concerned with the quite different sentences in which *his* (or *him*) and *Bill* both receive extra-heavy contrastive stress (such as might be heard if the sentences of (3) were shouted across the room at a noisy cocktail party or through a closed car window). Comparing these with (4),

(4) a. Bill criticized John's book, although Bill had not
        read it (taken it with him)(left it on the table).
    b. Bill knew John, although John had never met him.

we see that the Big Ender hypothesis is strongly confirmed, whereas the HSP receives no support whatever.[15] By the EW hypothesis,[16] the above

facts are accounted for in a quite natural and perfectly general way.[17]
To the HSPer the above facts are unjustified and are no more to be expected
than, say, if (4) were ungrammatical and (2) and (3) were grammatical.[18]

One might even speculate that the explanation for these facts is
to be found at a much deeper level where grammatical categories, Platonic
ideals, moral necessity, and *Sinn und Bedeutung* become indistinguishable,
and, hence, indiscernible. On this view, sentences are held together by
a kind of "nuclear glue" consisting of mesons, alpha-particles, and meaning
postulates, all swirling in more-or-less quantized orbits around an un-
differentiated plasma of feature bundles.[19] Thus, the earlier notion of
a grammar as an abstract yet concretely manifested generative-recognition
algorithm is abandoned, and is replaced by a device (to return to a more
traditional sense of that word) in which features specify and are specified
by other features in various combinations, subject, of course, to obvious
constraints which need not concern us here. Whatever else may be said in
favor of this position, it is at least unassailable, and this in itself
represents a significant advance in the Theory of Universal Grammar as this
field has traditionally been conceived. Opposed to this at the present
time stands only the Theory of Universal Derivational Constraints, which,
although it is likewise unassailable, suffers from a lack of plausibility.
To draw a not unapt analogy, the latter theory views a grammar as a machine
in which one inserts a fudgecicle and receives a dime in return.[20] Of
course, if for any reason the derivation is blocked, then the machine will
neither give a fudgecicle as output nor return the dime.[21] In general,
this will happen a countably infinite number of times on any given sentence
(rendering speech production an impossibility) although not in a manner
definable as a recursive function (which would reduce child language and
aphasia to absurdity), as can be shown by a straightforward argument *ad
rem*.[22] Coughlake makes what is perhaps the best possible argument in favor
of the Unsupportable Position when he says that derivational constraints
should be left unrestrained, since, he argues, they have been exploited
for too long already by non-derivational chauvinists attempting to exert
a kind of interpretivist imperialism, a *pax lexicalis* as it were, over the
realm of syntax. But on closer inspection this argument, too, is seen to
crumble when we consider the results of Bach and Busoni. The Bach-Busoni
Paradox[23] (often confused with the Burali-Forti Paradox, to which it bears
not the slightest resemblance) states that the restriction on transformational
rules are already overly permissive and that this allows a grammar to gene-
rate a lot of stuff that is, frankly, garbage.[24] Should this be allowed
to accumulate, transformational-generative grammar could reach an ecological
crisis, suffocating in its own effluvium. At the present time, until we
understand more about the neuroanatomy of the dolphin or until a chimpanzee
is taught to recite the "Hare Krishna" in Sledd's dialect, I see no way to
avoid vacuousness and triviality except by swearing fealty to the EW hypothesis and all that it entails (or presupposes). It is, after all, the
principal function of intellectuals to believe the Truth when it is identified to them as such.

NOTES

[1] David Cohen and Tony Robson read and commented on an earlier version
of this paper and suggested many changes, most of which I have ignored.
Although they might like to deny it, they cannot escape entirely the responsibility for any mistakes.

[2] See, for example, *Aspects of the Theory of Syntax, Syntactic Structures,* the 1955 Unpublished Manuscript, the paper at the Texas Conference, the stuff in the Bach-Harms volume, the three chapters in *Handbook of Mathematical Psychology,* although those are pretty hard, and of course all the underground mimeographed stuff, if you can get it, and all those red things from Harvard, and then of course there is *Linguistic Inquiry*; you should read all of *Linguistic Inquiry* whenever it comes out if you really want to keep up with what's going on. Listen, I know that a lot of it is crap, but you really should subscribe to it anyway. Here's a subscription blank for you to clip out and mail along with your check. (Be sure to read the footnote on the other side first).

> Yes! Rush me two years of *Linguistic Inquiry* at the special introductory rate of $30.00 (a saving of $15.00 over the newsstand price)! I understand that if I am not completely satisfied, I will not be alone.
>
> Name _____
>
> Address _____
>
> Institution _____
>
> Rank _____
>
> Where did you first hear of *Linguistic Inquiry*?_____

[3] See, for example, recent intemperate articles in the *Journal of Contrary Claims, Counterexamples, Refutations, Denials, Denunciations, Objections, Quibbles, Protests, Ripostes, Replies, Rejoinders, Repartee, and Recriminations:* the Permanent Press, daily.

[4] It was the Twelfth Century which impelled Lucius Beebe to exclaim, "I could pick a better century out of a hat!" Why Beebe felt so strongly about this particular century has never been satisfactorily explained.

[5] A lot more people (linguists, to take a notorious example) can "make out what it's about" in French than can actually <u>read</u> it.

[6] It was in fact the Twentieth Century that Beebe eventually picked out of a hat. Perhaps that helps to clear up some things you've been wondering about.

[7] See, for example, R. Mason Dixon, 'On what there seems to me to be', who seems to understand it perfectly. Yossarian (unpublished mimeo, M.I.T.) also understands it.

[8] I am indebted to J. R. Oss for suggesting this to me.

[9] Cf. Coughlake, "Why, as for me, do I dislike it masterfully that no one can ever speak the dialect as I have done so, too?" ideas delivered informally and somewhat incoherently to a gathering of linguists and miscellaneous gate-crashers at the Fifth Texas Conference on Methodological Preliminaries. The text was reconstructed from the mental notes of the par-

ticipants and is on file in the archives of the University of Texas Rare
Book Depository and Gunnery Range.

[10] The terms 'Little Ender' and 'Big Ender' ate taken from the well-known
factions in Swift's *Gulliver's Travels*, who quarreled incessantly and to
the point of occasional war over a proper point at which to break an egg.
Gulliver's spineless compromise solution to this dilemma is too drearily
familiar to warrant discussion here.

[11] Pious pronouncements such as "East, west, home's best", do not bear on
this much larger and intrinsically more interesting question.

[12] Beaver, Eager T.("Split"), 'Damn the rocky shoals of dust-bowl empiricism
and full steam ahead into the deep tranquil waters of unsubstantiated
speculation', mimeo, the Esalen Institute, about a year or so ago; it was
about so thick and it was in a manila envelope. It used to be in that stack
of stuff to be read. Perhaps you lent it to someone. But who?

[13] Those who think that it is a matter of definition probably couldn't
define *three* without resort to the Axiom of Choice.

[14] The *John* appearing (or, better, mentioned) in numerous linguistic
examples has been shown to be, in fact, John of Gaunt, the first man
to star a sentence he secretly suspected to be perfectly grammatical. The
identity of *Bill* remains a mystery, although some believe that it is
William Holden.

[15] Let's face it -- you're having a hard time following this. The examples
aren't too clear, and you can't remember anymore why the sentences of
(3) are supposed to be ungrammatical (if indeed they are), and besides, the
ones in (2), which are supposed to be grammatical don't look so hot either.
Moreover, even granting that the facts are correct, you don't see how the
conclusion follows from them, and you're not even sure that you care all
that much, although if you don't read the rest, some smart-ass is sure to
grill you on some obscure point in it, and you'll have to bluff your way
through again until you get a chance to really sit down and go over it
carefully to make sure you really understand what in hell is going on.
Look, maybe the thing to do would be to go into historical linguistics and
let syntax go for a while -- at least until things settle down a little
and these assholes stop printing every hare-brained hallucination that
afflicts their heads.

[16] I see you have decided to read on anyway, in the hope that it will all
be explained later.

[17] Bullshit! The reason I can cudgel you like this with *non sequiturs* is
that you are one of those people who wouldn't admit to yourself some
pages earlier that you really haven't any idea what is involved in a "verificationist" philosophy. Even granted that you came to this paper at a
disadvantage, still there is no excuse for how easy it is to intimidate
you into thinking that the arguments are too arcane for you to understand
with your merely human intelligence. However, with an audience like you,
there is no doubt that an attitude of militant self-assurance will suffice
to cover up almost any lack of cogency, however glaring.

[18] Which is probably, in fact, the case.

[19] If you had trouble with "Boolean conditions on analyzability", this one is going to keep you out in left field for some time.

[20] It has come to my attention that an ice cream machine must view its environment as just such a machine. I am indebted to the man who came to look at the plaster in the bedroom for this observation.

[21] People often wonder what happens to all the derivations that get blocked. You and I know that they don't go anywhere because they were never really derivations in the first place, but when you try to explain this to a beginning class in syntax, they always tend to get a bit edgy.

[22] This is pretty deep stuff. Unless, of course, you are a mathematician, in which case it's pretty trivial stuff, but you can't be too sure because you don't know anything about linguistics.

[23] See, Bach-Busoni, 'Paradoxes for the left hand alone; edited and transcribed into easy keys by Philip of Spain'; the text is written in binary and the pages are Gödel numbered, so it is not particularly easy to find things in this book. However, since the description of the Bach-Busoni Paradox is known to consist of no more than 23 words, it is possible, in principle, to locate it. "If it's there, we'll get to it eventually, but it might take a while," was the way one of our Turing machine operators put it.

[24] The disastrous results of letting grammars run wild, with no restraints whatever on their rules, is too well known to merit discussion here. Letting any string be replaced by any string whatever, even a shorter one (the null string in the worst cases), allowing transformations add and delete virtually anything at will, the liberal use of rule and exception features -- all these have started out as only "minor" modifications of the theory, just one little device here, a novel gimmick there, all plausibly argued for and justified on the basis of necessity at the time, but over the years they have accumulated into a licentious tangle of options and alternatives, and, predictably, they have led to "harder" stuff such as Derivational Constraints.

V. WHIMSY II

A CONTRIBUTION TO THE REPERTORY OF EXAMPLES

CHARLES J. FILLMORE
Ohio State University and
Center for Advanced Study in the Behavioral Sciences

A stacked relative clause construction (or, simply, a stacked relative) is a construction in which a relative clause modifies a nominal construction already containing a relative clause. A cleft sentence is a sentence one of whose constituents is introduced by anticipatory IT.[1] A sentence which exhibits simultaneously stackedness and cleavage is the following:

IT'S MY BUXOM COUSIN WHO'S WEARING A LOW-CUT SWEATER
THAT'S A GOOD EXAMPLE OF A CLEFT STACKED RELATIVE.

NOTE

[1] It's extremely important to distinguish cleft sentences from pseudo-cleft sentences. Instances of cleavage have IT in front; instances of pseudo-cleavage have WHAT in front.

POLYGLOSSOLALIA

Members of the LARYNX-HORN KAMMERCHOR*

"Why don't you sit here?" he suggested in Lapp.

"They can't draft me now!" he said in Kannaḍa.

"I'm going to go lie in the sun," he announced in Basque.

"That makes another $500 I owe you," he groaned in Dutch.

"What's a trayfer?" he inquired naïvely in Tocharian.[1]

"Down, Spot!" he commanded in Dalmatian.

"Too bad I can't castle now," K. said in Czech.

"I've never even <u>heard</u> of that position before!" she exclaimed in Fukinese.

"Up, up and away," I sang in my beautiful Walloon.

"Roquefort or Thousand Islands?" the waiter asked in Lettish.

"I'm teaching Fido a second language," he informed us in Miaou.

"What do you call a policeman in Pig Greek?" he asked in Koiné.

"Don't play cards with Black Bart," he warned in Ilichiti.

"What's this tough meat, waiter?" she asked in Dogrib.

"I wonder why the princess is spending so much time on those mattresses," he said grimly in Techachapi.

"I look stunning in this outfit," she said in Dotted Swiss. (sic)

"8 ball in the side pocket," he announced in Reverse English. (sic)

"We seem to have gotten ourselves into an untenable position," he said in Upper Creek. (siccer)

"I find myself totally immobilized," the Frenchman said in Cambodge.

"I shall go!" cried the Latin lover in Ibo.

"Go speak to Mr. Whosis," advised the Tanzanian in Fulani.

"Thanks," replied the other one in Asante.

"I can't seem to remember just <u>why</u> I went for a swin in the Lethe," she admitted in a Bolivian dialect.

"Why do they call him Old Yellowtooth?" he wondered in Tartar.

"This means sudden death!" the coach warned them in Thai.

"How do you spell 'precede'," he asked in Singhalese.

"ARRGGHHHH, they got me," he moaned in Ndebele.

"I just feel weak all over," she confessed in Mono.

"That laser beam sure took care of MIT!" the mad scientist cackled in Zapotec.

"You're confusing Musial with Yogi Berra," he said in Hindustani.

"Hey, Eenglish, I sell you my seester!" whispered the dirty little boy in Mon-Khmer. "You wanta virgin, you gotta pay extra," he added in Chasta-Costa.

"The hell with MyLai, how do I get to MyLou?" the grizzled colonel demanded in Shqip.

"Getcha red hot peanuts!" he cried in Venda.

"Schlitz, you should drink. Oy, That's the beer for ein real mensch!" he said in Hebrew.

"They just don't make 'em like Flo Nightingale anymore," the doctor sighed in Old Norse.

"I'm afraid I got another minos score," he admitted in Cretan.

"Sounds like a shady deal to me," he warned in Umbrian.

"Let me show you the rest of my microbus," he suggested suavely in Van. "I _do_ adore the paint job," she conceded in Teutonic.

"Can I come too?" asked her little brother in Tagalog.

"What do fools do where angels fear to go?" he wondered in Russian.

"What promise?" he sneered in Welsh.

"What is the purpose served by that long stick of wood?" asked the visiting dignitary in Tübatulabal.

"Overcome," they chanted in Huchol.

"Grfflggh," he muttered in Geg.

"Oy!" he said in Vey.[2]

NOTES

* These inanities and numerable others contrived by Dr. (Forthcoming)
Larynx-horn, with a little help from his friends: J & G Mañana-Verde
(now ill annoyed in Chambana-Urpain), G & R Lac Oeuf (the notorious Michi-
gander and -goose), New Ballpower, and -- lest but not least we forget --
that universal Quang-defier, the Festschriftee Himself.

[1] Explanations and translations upon available request.

[2] All rites preserved.

THE LINGUIST'S ALPHABET BOOK

ALBIN SCHRIMPUWSKIN

A   is for aegis and also for aye;

B   is for bdellium, I don't know why.

C   is for chthonian, cnidoblast and cue;

D   is for djinn, pence and Dneiper, too.

E   is for eye, for eau and for ewe;

F   is for ghoti that swim just like you.

H   is for honest, for honour and hue;

I   is for peace.

J   is for Jugoslavia.

K   is for knight and also for knosh;

L   is for llama, by golly, by gosh.

M   is for mnemonic and for mother, too;

N   is for nothing, I think -- don't you?

O   is for Oedipus and also for one;

P   for psychology, Ptolemy and pnumb.

Q   is for queue, and

R   for aardvaark, living in treeses;

S   is for See, and

T   is for tmesis!

U   is for all of us and

V   is for "five";

W   's for write and why and, moreover, wive.

X   is for xylophone, which no one would heist;

Y   is for yew, and

Z   for Zeitgeist.

FRAGMENTS FROM THE COLLECTIVE SUBCONSCIOUS:
A TENTATIVE RECONSTRUCTION[1]

FOM POP
University of Alberta

SCENE ONE: At Bills' House. As the curtain rises, we find BILL *and* HARRY *deep in conversation.*

BILL: I saw something that was horrible.[2]

HARRY: Yes?[3]

BILL: I saw John kissing Mary.[4]

HARRY: John?[5]

BILL: She nodded her approval.[6]

HARRY: He's a lucky fellow![7]   It'd make the time pass more quickly.[8]

BILL: John laid his plans very cleverly.[9]   He was driven on by his love of power.[10]

HARRY: John is easy to please.[11]

BILL: John annoyed Mary with his persistence.[12] Mary began to doubt John's intentions.[13] She had a curious sinking of the heart.[14] John loosened Mary's dress.[15]

HARRY: Nobody that I know has ever done anything like that.[16]

BILL: Mary pinched John's nose.[16] John stopped![17] He turned hostile.[18] They fought tooth and nail.[19] Never had I seen such a fight.[20] John injured himself by hitting himself on the head with a hammer.[21]

HARRY: One hardly knows what to say.[22]

BILL: He suffered a severe shock.[23] She was weeping.[24] Streams of tears gushed out of her eyes, and the greatness of her grief rent her heart in sunder.[25] She screamed herself into a fit.[26] She rubbed her cheeks with her two clenched fists and ran to open the door.[27]

HARRY: Then what?[28]

BILL: John left, and he didn't even say goodbye.[29]

HARRY: John was clever in leaving early.[30]

BILL: He ran away because he was afraid.[31]   When John ran away we went home.[32]

HARRY: John is unlikely to run for Congress.[33]

JOHN (*off*): Open the door![34]

HARRY: John has arrived.[35]

BILL (*to John*): I don't see how you can be proud of what you have done.[36] GO AWAY I DON'T WANT TO TALK WITH YOU ANY MORE TODAY.[37] We want no undesirables around here.[38] I know you won't let us down.[39]

HARRY: John thinks he is smarter than he is.[40] Has he gone?[41] What will he do?[42]

BILL: Naturally John will leave.[43]

HARRY: No, I'm afraid he won't.[44] He does not fear me.[45]

BILL: John won't go, will he?[46]

HARRY: I do not know.[47] He said so, but I doubt it.[48]

BILL: Oh![49]

THE CURTAIN FALLS with the outcome of the situation uncertain.

SCENE TWO: At John's mother's house. The curtain rises on a scene of considerable agitation: JOHN'S MOTHER, arms akimbo, is interrogating HARRY.

JOHN'S MOTHER: Did John come?[50]

HARRY: Yes.[51] I told him to come on time.[52] He said nothing, and what is is worse, laughed at us.[53] John tried to hit Bill.[54]

J. M.: Why else would he have come?[55]

HARRY: He wounded himself.[56] In the ear.[57] I besought John to leave.[58]

J. M.: Poor John.[59]

HARRY: I should like to know how and why he did it.[60]

J. M.: He hot-footed it home.[61] John is here.[62]

HARRY: Does John live here?[63]

J. M.: Yes![64] The police brought him in.[65] They are elsewhere.[66] John appears ill.[67] He got weaker and weaker until he could lift hardly more than five pounds.[68]

HARRY: Good Gracious! Is he dead?[69]

J. M.: He is to a certain extent.[70] Homo est mortalis.[71]

HARRY: Does John have a chance to live?[72]

J. M.: John is having a banana split.[73]

HARRY: The man is sick.[74] There is something about it that puzzles me.[75]

J. M.: Huh?[76]

HARRY: Is it common for people to act that way?[77] How do you feel about it?[78]

J. M.: Well, boys will be boys.[79]

HARRY: This statement is based on error.[80] Don't be an ass![81]

J. M.: Be quiet![82] Poor John sleeps.[83]

HARRY: If I was rude I apologize.[84] I beg your pardon.[85]

J. M.: Granted![86]

HARRY: John is a donkey.[87] He pretended to be holy.[88] John was the one that struck Bill.[89]

J. M.: John's having hit Bill made sense;[90] a breeze loosened Mary's dress.[91]

HARRY: His excuse was pitifully weak.[92] John hurt Mary;[93] Mary is ill.[94] It often happens in these cases that the wise are unfortunate and the fools are successful.[95] Un crime si horrible merite la mort.[96]

J. M.: John is stupid and Bill and Harry are similar.[97]

CURTAIN

NOTES[1]

[1] With the recent dramatic increase in published linguistic material, it has now become possible to start piecing together that Universal Discourse which is vouchsafed in whole to none, but in part to many. See also my embryonic article, 'The non-arbitrariness of the linguistic example', to be published lengthily.

[2] Emmon Bach (1968).
[3] David Abercrombie (1967).
[4] Henry Gleason (1955).
[5] Benjamin Elson and Velma Pickett (1962).
[6] Otto Jespersen (1937).
[7] Leonard Bloomfield (1917).
[8] Paul Garvin (1962).
[9] Noam Chomsky (1965).
[10] R. H. Robins (1964).
[11] Jerrold J. Katz (1963).

[12] Robert A. Hall (1965).
[13] Frederick Newmeyer (1969).
[14] Vilém Mathesius (1928).
[15] George Lakoff (1965).
[16] Charles J. Fillmore (1967).
[17] C. E. Bazell (1962).
[18] M. A. K. Halliday (1967).
[19] Jespersen (1937).
[20] Fillmore (1967).
[21] Lakoff (1965).
[22] Bloomfield (1933).
[23] Halliday (1967).
[24] Gleason (1955).
[25] John Smith (1657).
[26] Jespersen (1937).
[27] M. A. K. Halliday, Angus McIntosh, and Peter Strevens (1964).
[28] Elson and Pickett (1962)
[29] John R. Ross (1967).
[30] Lakoff (1965).
[31] Jespersen (1937).
[32] Bloomfield (1931).
[33] Anthony L. Vanek (1970).
[34] James D. McCawley (1968).
[35] Chomsky (1952).
[36] Serge Karcevskij (1931).
[37] Charles F. Hockett (1958).
[38] Dwight L. Bolinger (1968).
[39] J. R. Firth (1935).
[40] McCawley (196?).
[41] Zellig Harris (1946).
[42] Elson and Pickett (1962).
[43] Chomsky (1965).
[44] P. H. Matthews (1967).
[45] Joshua Whatmough (1956).
[46] Gleason (1955).
[47] Louis Hjelmslev (1943), trans. Whitfield (1953).
[48] Rulon Wells (1945).
[49] William Dwight Whitney (1875).
[50] Matthews (1967).
[51] Hockett (1958).
[52] L.R. Micklesen (1956).
[53] Jespersen (1937).
[54] Newmeyer (1969).
[55] Ross (1967).
[56] Paul Chapin (1967).
[57] N. S. Trubetzkoy (1958), trans. Baltaxe (1969).
[58] Lakoff (1965).
[59] Henri Frei (1956).
[60] Jespersen (1937).
[61] Bloomfield (1933).
[62] Gleason (1955).
[63] William Moulton (1966).
[64] Abercrombie (1963).
[65] Chomsky (1962).

[66] E. Colin Cherry, Morris Halle, and Roman Jakobson (1953).
[67] Robert Binnick (1970).
[68] Edward Sapir (1944).
[69] Jespersen (1937).
[70] Daniel Jones (1909).
[71] Franz Bopp (1816).
[72] Chomsky (1962).
[73] Binnick (1970).
[74] Franz Boas (1911).
[75] Jerry A. Fodor and Jerrold J. Katz (1963).
[76] André Martinet (1960).
[77] Hockett (1958).
[78] Ferdinand de Saussure (1915), trans. Baskin (1959).
[79] Hockett (1958).
[80] Bach (1964).
[81] Firth (1951).
[82] Matthews (1967).
[83] Jehoshua Bar-Hillel (1964).
[84] Bernard Bloch (1947).
[85] Martinet (1960).
[86] Alan Palmer (1932).
[87] Hermann Paul (1890), trans. Strong.
[88] Joseph Priestley (1762).
[89] Lakoff (1965).
[90] Newmeyer (1969).
[91] Lakoff (196?).
[92] Rodney D. Huddleston (1967).
[93] L. M. Myers (1952).
[94] Willem de Groot (1956).
[95] Aristotle (880 B.C.).
[96] Claude Lancelot and Antoine Arnaud (1660).
[97] McCawley (1968).

NOTES ON NOTES

[1] For the sake of brevity[1] only the date of publication[2] is given.

NOTES ON [NOTES ON NOTES]

[1] and laziness.

[2] or manuscripture or duplication.

WELL DONNE

Dr. FORTHCOMING LARYNX-HORN

From the description of islands given by J. R. Ross in his dissertation (1967), it follows that (2), although it is apparently a natural continuation of a discourse begun by (1), is nevertheless ungrammatical.

(1) Michigan isn't a good place to study linguistics.

(2) *Then **what** _is_ it a good place to study?

As Ross observes, such structures as "a good place to study X" form islands, and the "X" cannot be moved out, as it is in (2). On the other hand, the absence of an island in (3), together with the fact that preposition-stranding is permissible in English, permit the movement resulting in (4):

(3) Ann Arbor isn't a good place for linguistics.

(4) What _is_ Ann Arbor a good place for?

Now, consider the sentence

(5) Sam is no man for that job.

As we have seen, (5) cannot be grammatically questioned by

(6) *For what job is Sam no man?

This fact, while predicted by Ross (1967), results from the earlier research of J. Donne (1624) on this phenomenon, as expressed in his insightful observation that

(7) No man is an island.

REFERENCES

Donne, J. (1624) _Devotions_ XVII.

Ross, John Robert. (1967) _Constraints on Variables in Syntax_. Unpublished Ph.D. Thesis, Massachusetts Institute of Technology.

VI. PARODY AND BURLESQUE II: WIDER HORIZONS

EIGENVALUES IN GRAMMAR

CORA K. RICKULUM
University of Michigan

1. Commutative languages

A commutative language is a language which contains all permutations of every word in the language. The commutative closure L^c of a language L, is defined to be the smallest commutative language which contains L. It is easy to show that there are regular languages L such that L^c is not regular. For if we take L as $\{(01)^n | n > 1\}$, then, clearly, L is regular, but L^c is the set of all strings which have the same number of 0's and 1's, which is easily shown to be non-regular.[1]

Commutative languages have been studied previously by Chomsky and Schützenberger(1963) and by Fischer, Meyer and Rosenberg (1967). In the latter paper it is proved that the commutative languages are semilinear; that is, they are the finite unions of linear sets. We are thus justified in restricting our attention to commutative linear grammars.

Curiously, the cited authors have failed to notice the importance of eigenvalues in the study of commutative languages.

It is well known that a grammar can be represented by a set of equations, each of which has on the left a nonterminal symbol, and on the right the sum of the expansions of that symbol. For example, the grammar

$$S \rightarrow a\,A$$

$$S \rightarrow b$$

$$A \rightarrow b\,S$$

$$A \rightarrow a$$

can be expressed as

$$S = a\,A + b$$

$$A = b\,S + a$$

Using the methods of Chomsky (1963), these equations can be solved to obtain

$$S = (b + a^2)(1 - ab)^{-1}$$

However, we are concerned here not with solving the grammar but with finding its associated eigenvalues.

The equations of a linear commutative grammar are linear equations which can be represented in the general form

$$C\ X = X_0$$

where C is a square matrix of size n, X is a vector of size n composed of nonterminal symbols, and X_0 is a vector of size n composed of terminal symbols. For example, we have

$$\begin{vmatrix} 1 & -a \\ -b & 1 \end{vmatrix} \begin{pmatrix} S \\ A \end{pmatrix} = \begin{pmatrix} b \\ a \end{pmatrix}$$

The eigenvalues of the matrix C are obtained by setting

$$C\ X = \lambda\ X$$

and solving for λ. In the particular example we have

$$S - a\ A = \lambda\ S$$

$$A - b\ S = \lambda\ A.$$

The values of λ can be found by setting the determinant of $|C - \lambda\ I|$ equal to 0.

$$\begin{vmatrix} 1-\lambda & -a \\ -b & 1-\lambda \end{vmatrix} = 0$$

Evaluating we obtain $(1 - \lambda)^2 = a\ b$, hence $\lambda = 1 \pm \sqrt{ab}$.

The eigenvectors of the grammar, that is, the values for X in the equation

$$C\ X = \lambda\ X$$

can now be found. For the example, we obtain the values $S = 1$ and $A = \pm \sqrt{b/a}$, so the eigenvectors are $(\sqrt{a}, \sqrt{b})$ and $(\sqrt{a}, -\sqrt{b})$ and of course all scalar multiples of these vectors.

We conjecture, although we have as yet no proof, that in general the eigenvalues of a commutative grammar are real.

NOTE

[1] That commutative languages are the appropriate model for many natural languages was pointed out to us by a colleague. In particular, some Uto-Aztecan and Athabascan languages seem to be free-word-order languages.

REFERENCES

Fischer, P.C., A.R. Meyer, and A.L. Rosenberg. (1967) Real time counter languages. Yorktown Heights, N.Y.: IBM Research RC 1916.

Schützenberger, M.P. and N. Chomsky. (1963) The algebraic theory of context-free languages. In *Computer Programming and Formal Systems*, eds. Braffort and Hirschberg. Amsterdam: North-Holland. 118-161.

ON THE HISTORICAL SOURCE OF
SANCTIAN LINGUISTICS[1]

W. KEITH PERCIVAL

The question of the historical antecedents of the linguistic theory of the Spanish humanist Franciscus Sanctius Brocensis (Francisco Sánchez de las Brozas) has recently been unexpectedly illuminated by a discovery whose momentous importance has yet to be appreciated by historians of linguistics. I refer to the publication in Belém, Brazil by Professor Damião de Oliveira of substantial portions of a vast compendium of human knowledge by the little known Paduan humanist Bartolomeo Barbaro, who from 1535 to 1552 taught the trivium at the court of João III in Lisbon and Evora. Barbaro's work, which is impressively entitled *De omni scibili libri quadraginta: seu Prodromus pansophiae* [Forty books concerning all that is knowable: or the advanced guard of omniscience],[2] was written after Barbaro's arrival in Portugal and circulated widely in court circles in a number of manuscript copies.

Professor de Oliveira daringly conjectures that a printed edition of the work also existed, basing this supposition on a brief reference to it in an extremely rare Portuguese edition of Raffaele Maffei's monumental encyclopedia *Commentarii Urbani* (Coimbra, 1599).[3] After an extensive search of the bibliographical literature I have found only one reference to Barbaro's book, namely in Alfonso Ulloa's celebrated *Bibliografia das obras impressas em Portugal no século XVI* (Evora, 1901). Ulloa recalls (p. 110, fn. 3) having seen Barbaro's book mentioned in an unpublished manuscript by the Spanish humanist Juán Lopez de Castañeda (1580-1644), who regrets that he has been unable to find a single copy of it in any library in Spain. But this remark does not, of course, prove the existence of a printed edition.

The existence of a manuscript edition, on the other hand, is now a well established fact thanks to the tireless efforts of Professor de Oliveira. How many copies were made of the work is, however, a question which still remains in doubt. Professor de Oliveira was able to consult an all but complete copy in the private library of the Duc de Penthièvre in Paris and he has discovered several substantial fragments in libraries in Southern Europe and Latin America.

One such fragmentary manuscript is of special interest to historians of linguistics in that its first owner was none other than Franciscus Sanctius. It constitutes the whole of book I of the section of Barbaro's book devoted to the liberal arts, and is entitled *Summa perutilis in regulas distinctas totius artis grammatices*. The incipit reads as follows: Cogitanti mihi et tentanti saepe et curiosè qua uia possent facilius proficere pueri in arte grammatica ut, si fieri posset, confusio Babylonica funditùs è medio tolleretur. . . (fol. 1^R), and the work ends as follows: Expliciunt regule grammaticales Barptolemaei Barbari Patauini: uale candide lector et me ama ut debes (fol 44^V).

The manuscript consists of 44 leaves of parchment and is tastefully bound in vellum. Leaves are numbered in roman figures preceded by *fo.*, the collation is as follows: a - e⁸, f⁴ numbers in signatures being also roman. The first owner's signature is in the top left-hand corner of the first left recto; it reads *Fremcisquo Sanches das Broças* and is followed by the date 1538 in roman numbers. Professor de Oliveira found this copy in the Museo Diocesano in Novara, Italy. It was acquired by the Museo in 1703 from a certain Gianfrancesco dei Fanteselli who was apostolic secretary to Pope Innocent XII. How the manuscript came into the possession of Fanteselli is not known.

About Sanctius' early life we know the following.[4] In 1534 at the age of eleven he was sent to Lisbon and for a number of years he served as a page to Queen Caterina and King João III. He then taught grammar and rhetoric to various members of the court until 1545, in which year he moved to Salamanca where he lived for the rest of his life. It is clear that Sanctius knew Barbaro and it is highly probable that he acquired his basic orientation to grammatical theory from him. This supposition is amply borne out by the portion of Barbaro's *Summa perutilis* which Professor de Oliveira reprints.

To make this great discovery more widely accessible I have obtained Professor de Oliveira's permission to transcribe the whole of folio 35 recto and part of folio 35 verso of the manuscript of the *Summa*, and to translate this entire passage into English.[5] The words and phrases in parentheses are interlinear notes in Sanctius' own hand. I have placed such material immediately to the right of the word or words over which it appeared in the manuscript.

The hand is a very angular variety of the *cancellaresca corsiva* rather reminiscent of the late fifteenth-century Florentine style. Sanctius, on the other hand, uses the *lettera antiqua tonda*, which is a great deal more difficult to read than the hand of the manuscript itself. I have left the spelling and punctuation unchanged except for the occasional ligatures and abbreviations, which are spelled out in full.

Modesty bids me refrain from commenting upon the substance of Sanctius' notes, his extreme youth offering a sufficient explanation for their impropriety. I reproduce them here purely in the interests of scientific objectivity.

Readers interested in the history of linguistics will notice a number of clear indications in the text presented here of notions which were to play a crucial role in Sancius' later grammatical method as expounded in his renowned *Minerva: seu de causis linguae Latinae*.[6]

For instance, Barbaro was fully aware of the distinction between surface structure (*vox*) and deep structure (*sensus*), and underscored their noncongruence. He also emphasized the close connexion of language and mind which had been all but completely ignored in the previous century. (Indeed the relation between the two was explicitly denied by Pescennio Negri in his influential *Modus epistulandi*).[7] It is clear also that Barbaro conceived of deep structure in semantic, not syntactic terms, in which respect his view of the nature of language is in advance of the one prevalent at the time.

Moreover, Barbaro operates with the notion of subaudition; that is, when necessary he posits understood elements not present in the surface structure. Since no examples occur in the text below I quote the following (fol. 16^V):

> Quot modis nominatiuus ante uerbum uenustè subticetur? Tribus. primo: In omni uerbo primae uel secundae personae potest nominatiuus subaudiri. Vt; scribo librum: intelligitur ego scribo.

> English translation: In how many ways is a nominative elegantly omitted before a verb? In three ways. First, in any verb of the first or second persons a nominative can be understood,e.g. *scribo librum* '(I) am writing a book' where *ego scribo* 'I am writing' is understood.

Finally it may be pointed out that Barbaro makes extensive use of the concept of syntactic figure (*figura constructionis*), which he explicitly attributes to the Stoic rhetorician Domitius Afer (circa 10 B.C. - 50 A.D.)[8] Portions of Afer's *Dialogi contra grammatistas* are, it may be recalled, quoted at length in the *De amphibologia* of Nonius Marcellus (ed. Habicht, pp. 625-632), and also in the elaborate linguistic commentary of Terrence's *Heautontimorumenos* by Velius Longus (ed. Tischendorff, vol. 2, pp. cxii-cxix passim).

Barbaro's definition of syntactic figure reads as follows: Figura constructionis est anomalia seu inaequalitas partium orationis facta cum ratione: necessitatis ornatusque gratia permissa 'A syntactic figure is a justifiable irregularity or incongruence among parts of speech sanctioned by reason of necessity or elegance' (fol. 10^R). This may be compared with the analogous definition at the beginning of the fourth book of Sanctius' *Minerva:* Figurae Constructionis sunt anomalia siue inaequalitas partium quae fit per Defectum, per Exuperationem, per Discordiam, per Inuersum ordinem 'Syntactic figures are an irregularity or incongruence among parts (of speech) resulting from omission, addition, substitution (?), or reversal of order' (fol. 164^R). Clearly Sanctius has plagiarized part of Barbaro's definition.[9] Moreover, the definition of syntactic figure in Afer's *Dialogi* in turn furnished the prototype for Barbaro: Figura est vitium factum cum ratione necessitatis causa vel ornatus 'A figure is a justifiable grammatical error committed because of necessity or elegance' (Habicht, p. 629; Tischendorff, p. cxv). Thus, the historical antecedents of Sanctius' theory of figures are clear.[10]

The reader not familiar with Renaissance Latin should note the following orthographical peculiarities:

    1. Confusion of *ae, oe,* and *e.* Thus *que* for *quae, faetet* for *fetet, teter* for *taeter.*
    2. No distinction between *u* and *v.* Both Sanctius and the scribe use *V* for the upper case, and *u* for the lower case. Hence *uox* for *vox, Vlysses* for *Ulysses, ut* but *Vt.*
    3. Inconsistent capitalization and punctuation. Thus *penelope* but *Dido.*
    4. *Loquutio* for *locutio* 'speech'.

EXTRACT FROM THE SUMMA PERUTILIS OF
BARTOLOMEO BARBARO

[fol. 35^R]

Quid est grammatica? loquutionis ratio et cogitationis.

Quid est loquutio? Rerum per humanam uocem significatio, ut cogitationes loquentis ab auditore concipiuntur.

Vnde ducitur loquutionis copia? Non aliunde quàm a cogitationis copia: naturam enim a principio quasi parem legem ubertatis dixisse liquet loquenti atque cogitanti.

Quid est constructio? debita dispositio partium orationis in ipsa oratione.

Constructionum quae est congrua sensu, et uoce? phyllis sedet (faetet).

Que sensu, et non uoce? populus currunt (pedunt). Turba ruunt (crepant).

Quae uoce, et non sensu? fides iacebant (pedebant).

Nominatiuus cum uerbo in quot debet concordare? in duobus, in numero, et in persona. Vt ego amo (pedo), tu amas (pedis), ille amat (pedit).

Adiectiuum cum substantiuo | [fol. 35^V] in quot debet concordare? in tribus. In numero, casu, et genere. ut Vlysses astutus (flatus teter), penelope pudica (merda odorifera), cornu sinistrum (peditum intempestiuum).

Relatiuum cum antecedente in quot debet concordare? In duobus: in numero, et in genere. Vt, Aeneas (crepitus) qui. Dido que. Ilium (peditum) quod.

Quare non conuenit relatiuum in persona? Quia relatiua omnia sicut adiectiua deficiunt persona, sed simulac antecedenti adhaeserint, persona se induunt antecedentis, Vt ego qui lego (micturio), tu qui legis (micturis), Iulius qui legit (micturit), eodem modo adiectiua sequuntur substantiua, ut ego Bartolemeus Barbarus Patauinus (Franciscus Sanctius Brocensis) doceo (disco) Olyssipone et Aeborae, Tu cynicus studiosus componis (cacaturis), Ille puer probus legit (crepat clare rubentibus auriculis).

ENGLISH TRANSLATION

What is grammar? The principles of speech and thought.[11]

What is speech? The designation of things by means of the human voice in such a manner that the thoughts of the speaker are understood by the hearer.

What is the origin of the fecundity of speech?[12] None

other than the fecundity of thought, for it is clear that from
the very outset nature imposed the same rule of fecundity on both
speech and thought.

What is syntax? The appropriate arrangement of parts
of speech in sentences.

What is an example of a construction which is congruent
in meaning and in surface structure? Phyllis is seated (stinks).

Another congruent in meaning and not in surface structure?
The people run (break wind). The crowd rush (break wind noisily).

Another congruent in surface structure and not in meaning?
The lyre was lying (breaking wind).[13]

In how many [categories] does a nominative agree with a
verb? In two [categories]: in number and person, e.g. I love
(break wind), he loves (breaks wind).

In how many [categories] does an adjective agree with a
noun? In three [categories]: in number, case, and gender, e.g.
artful Ulysses (a noisome breaking of wind), chaste Penelope
(fragrant excrement), left horn (an inopportune breaking of wind).

In how many [categories] does a relative agree with the
antecedent? In two [categories]: in number and gender, e.g.
Aeneas (a breaking of wind) who, Dido who, Troy (a breaking of
wind) which.

Why does the relative not agree in person? Because all
relatives like adjectives lack person. However, as soon as they
occur next to an antecedent they acquire the person of the antecedent, e.g. I who am reading (going to make water), thou who art
reading (going to make water), Julius who is reading (going to
make water). In the same manner adjectives follow nouns, e.g.
I Bartolomeo Barbaro, a Paduan (Franciscus Sanctius, a Brocensian)
teach (study) in Lisbon and Evora; thou cynical student art
writing (desirest to go to stool); he, well-behaved youth, is
reading (is breaking wind resoundingly, his ears reddening with
shame).

NOTES

[1] The term *grammatica Sanctiana* seems to have been coined by Caspar
Schoppe and, as far as I am aware, was first used in an essay entitled
'De veteris ac novae grammaticae Latinae origine, dignitate et usu,' which
he prefaced to his *Grammatica philosophica*, first published in Milan in
1628 (Amsterdam: Judocus Pluymer, 1659, sig. **2^V). This occurs in the
notorious passage in which Schoppe compares *grammatica Sanctiana* with what
he calls *grammatica cloacina* 'sewer-pipe grammar', i.e., grammatical theory
of the type which prevailed before the advent of Sanctian grammar!

[2] The full reference of Professor de Oliveira's publication is as follows:

Damião de Oliveira (ed.), *Bartholomaei Barbari De Omni Scibili Libri Quad-raginta: seu Prodromus Pansophiae.* Belém: Tip. da Emprêsa nacional de publicidade, 1966. Pp. xxiv, 368. This tastefully produced edition contains an extremely able introduction by Professor de Oliveira, followed by the text of the Penthièvre manuscript, books 25 to 30 (pp. 1-208). These are devoted to arithmetic, geometry, astronomy, and music. What follows then are the books on the trivium (grammar, dialectic, and rhetoric) in the version of the Fanteselli manuscript (pp. 209-310). Finally Professor de Oliveira reproduces the text of a single book entitled *Theatrum Hermeticum et Chymicum Mercuriophili Lusitani*, devoted to alchemy.

[3] The passage, according to Professor de Oliveira (p. xi) reads as follows: 'O livro primeiro do Prodromus de Bartolomeo Barbaro, impresso em Coimbra em 1541 por Abraham aben Usque, é uma obra excessivamente rara,' this statement allegedly occurring on sig. 2F5[R] of the 1599 Coimbra edition of Maffei's *Commentarii*. I have not been able to verify this citation.

[4] Our only source of information on Sanctius' childhood and youth is the *Pericope genealogica da Familia Sanches das Broças, fielmente compilada pelo Visconde de Sanches de Brito*, Lisboa: Typ. da Casa Minerva, 1698, p. 39.

[5] I should like to make it clear that I do not propose my translations of Barbaro as in any sense definitive. They are provided merely to aid the reader to a more rapid and painless comprehension of the text.

[6] Sanctius' magnum opus first appeared in 1587 in Salamanca, and was printed by the Renaut brothers. A little known fact is that a *Vorstudie* of the *Minerva* appeared in 1579 (Lyon, Gryphius) entitled *Organum grammaticale cunctis disciplinis utilissimum ac necessarium*. Copies of this earlier work are extremely rare. The only one I am aware of at the present time is in a small library in provincial Argentina, namely the Biblioteca del ministerio de guerra y marina, in San Salvador de Jujuy.

[7] The *Modus epistulandi* appeared in Venice in 1488,see *Jöchers Allgemeine Gelehrtenlexicon*, 8. Ergänzungsband, col. 1948. The book is curiously enough not mentioned in the *Gesamtkatalog der Wiegendrucke*. However, information about Negri can be found in Mario Cosenza, *Dictionary of the Italian Humanists*, vol. 3, p. 2469 under the rubric Niger, Pescennius Franciscus. Negri's statement about the relation of language and thought reads as follows: Cogitationum copiam verborum copiam non gignere omnibus peritis rerum grammaticarum satis claret. This occurs in a passage in which Negri indulges in a long tirade against Cicero and imitators of Cicero, and it seems specifically aimed at the statement in *De Oratore* (3,31,125) to the effect that rerum copia verborum copiam gignit. See in this connexion Giandomenico Cavalcanti, *Storia del Ciceronianismo*, Vigevano, 1864, p. 65.

[8] It is strange that Barbaro does not refer to the discussion of *verborum figurae* in Quintilian 9,3,1, to which he seems to owe much more than he does to Domitius Afer's work.

[9] That Sanctius was an inveterate plagiarist was pointed out in the last

century by Manfred Tunzelmann von Adlerflug in a carefully documented
study entitled *Das literarische Plagiat im Zeitalter der Renaissance,*
Halle, 1883. See especially pp. 960-987.

[10] It should be recalled at this point that Domitius Afer is known to have
been an especially unoriginal writer. He seems to have got the bulk
of his ideas from Poseidonius of Apamaea (circa 135-51 B.C.). On Poseidonius' influence on Roman philosophers and rhetoricians see Horst Erbse,
*Überlieferungsgeschichte der hellenistischen Literatur in der früheren
Kaiserzeit,* Giessen: Frühauf Verlag, 1932.

[11] It is hard for a modern reader to appreciate the revolutionary character
of this definition contrasting as it does so sharply with the traditional *grammatica est ars recte loquendi* 'grammar is the art of speaking
correctly'. Strangely enough it is the traditional definition which
Sanctius adopts and not Barbaro's, see *Minerva,* fol. 9R.

[12] The concept conveyed by the term *copia* 'fulness, abundance, fertility'
is very close to the modern notion of the creative aspect of language
use, see Berthold La Rue von Kleinmuth,*Ansätze zu einer notwendigen Sprach-
lehre auf transformationeller Grundlage nebst eine bündige Einleitung in
die allgemeine Grammatik,* Münster: Verlag Furzheim , 1970.

[13] The semantic incongruence in this sentence for Barbaro consists in the
fact that *fides* 'lyre' is a plural noun and as such agrees with the
third person plural verb *iacebant*'were lying', whereas semantically *fides*
is singular and is not appropriate to a plural verb. Note that it was the
subject which was said to agree with the verb, and not vice versa.

ZWEI BISHER UNBEKANNTE AS. RANDGLOSSEN

JOSEPH B. VOYLES
University of Washington

Mehrmals in der Handschriftenforschung der altdeutschen Dialekte sind Randglossen humoristischen Inhalts zur Kenntnis der Wissenschaft gekommen (z.B., Wolfgang Stammler, Ein Rätsel als Blattfüllsel, *Zeitschrift für deutsche Philologie* 54:377 (1929)). Ich bin der Überzeugung, zwei ähnliche Glossen humoristischer Art in der Handschrift der Trierer Pflanzen-, Fisch- und Alphabet-Glossen gefunden zu haben (für eine vollständigere Analyse der Handschrift vgl. Otto B. Schlutter, Altenglisch-Althochdeutsches aus dem Codex Trevirensis No. 40, *Anglia* 35:145-54 (1912)). Diese Blattfüllsel sind kleine vierzeilige Rätsel in einem älteren niederdeutschen (wahrscheinlich spät-as.) Dialekt. Die Zeilen befinden sich auf den ersten zwei Blättern der Handschrift (Bl. 1 und Bl. 2), je eine Zeile oben rechts nd unten links auf der Vorderseite jedes Blattes und je eine Zeile oben links und unten rechts auf der Kehrseite desselben Blattes. Jede Zeile ist ganz oben bzw. unten mit einer sehr feinen Handschrift geschrieben, worauf wir in aller Wahrscheinlichkeit die Tatsache zurückführen können, dass die Zeilen von der bisherigen Forschung unbeachtet blieben. Interessant ist die Verwendung einer in den as. Glossen üblichen Geheimschrift (vgl. J.H. Gallée, *Altsächsische Grammatik*, 2. Auflage, Halle, 1910, S. 13) in der letzten Zeile jedes Rätsels, wobei statt des Vokals, der im Alphabet folgende Konsonant geschrieben wird.

Die zwei Rätsel (mit meiner Übersetzung) sind:

Bl. 1 (Vorderseite, dann Kehrseite):

(r, oben rechts)	cnoc cnoc [knok knok]	(onomatopöetisch, das Klopfen an einer Tür)
(v, unten links)	hwie is thar [hwīə is ðar]	Wer ist da?
(r, oben links)	en mahgt [ɛn máxt]	Eine Magd.
(v, unten rechts)	nfn mbchtb .ck sfbn [nɛn máxt ik sean]	(d.h., nen machta ick sean) Niemand konnte ich sehen.

Bl. 2 (Vorderseite, dann Kehrseite):

(r, oben rechts)	cnoc cnoc	(das Klopfen)
(v, unten links)	hwie thar	Wer da?
(r, oben links)	en mahg [ēn máx]	Ein Verwandter.
(v, unten rechts)	n. mbh .c mbgb [ni máx ik maga]	(d.h., ni mah ic maga) Ich mag Verwandte nicht.

199

Der Humor besteht anscheinend darin, dass der Verfasser in den zwei
letzten Zeilen in jedem der Witze zwei völlig oder doch beinahe homophone
Wörter angesetzt hat.